The New Financial Deal

Understanding the Dodd-Frank Act and Its (*Unintended*) Consequences

David Skeel

WILEY

John Wiley & Sons, Inc.

Published by John Wiley & Sons, Inc., Hoboken, New Jersey.
Published simultaneously in Canada.

Limit of Liability/Disclaimer of Warranty: While the publisher and author have used
their best efforts in preparing this book, they make no representations or warranties
with respect to the accuracy or completeness of the contents of this book and specifically
disclaim any implied warranties of merchantability or fitness for a particular purpose. No
warranty may be created or extended by sales representatives or written sales materials.
The advice and strategies contained herein may not be suitable for your situation. You
should consult with a professional where appropriate. Neither the publisher nor author
shall be liable for any loss of profit or any other commercial damages, including but not
limited to special, incidental, consequential, or other damages.

For general information on our other products and services or for technical support, please
contact our Customer Care Department within the United States at (800) 762-2974,
outside the United States at (317) 572-3993 or fax (317) 572-4002.

Wiley also publishes its books in a variety of electronic formats. Some content that appears
in print may not be available in electronic books. For more information about Wiley
products, visit our web site at www.wiley.com.

Library of Congress Cataloging-in-Publication Data:
Skeel, David, 1961–
      The new financial deal : understanding the Dodd-Frank act and its (unintended)
consequences / David Skeel.
         p.   cm.
      Includes bibliographical references and index.
      ISBN 978-0-470-94275-8 (cloth); ISBN 978-1-118-01490-5 (ebk);
      ISBN 978-1-118-01491-2 (ebk); ISBN 978-1-118-01492-9 (ebk);
    1. United States. Dodd-Frank Wall Street Reform and Consumer Protection Act.
2. Financial services industry—Law and legislation—United States.   3. Financial
institutions—Law and legislation—United States.   I. Title.
      KF969.58201A2   2010
      346.73'08—dc22
                                                                        2010042162

Printed in the United States of America

10 9 8 7 6 5 4 3 2 1

For H.P., T.G., and B.B.

Contents

Part III   The Future

Foreword

September 15, 2008, was a day of infamy for the global financial markets. The increasing financial stress precipitated by a free-fall subprime mortgage crisis, and fueled by excessive risk taking and greed, exploded. At approximately 2:00 A.M. of that day, at the virtual insistence of the U.S. Treasury, the Federal Reserve System, and the Securities and Exchange Commission, Lehman Brothers Holdings Inc., the fourth largest U.S. investment bank, with extensive international operations, filed a Chapter 11 bankruptcy case. This unleashed a tsunami that threatened to destroy the worldwide financial system. The bankruptcy of the Lehman enterprise has produced a plethora of articles, books, strange bedfellows, and all types of political intrigue and deal making.

David Skeel has entered the stage to succinctly focus sunlight on the events that occurred and resulted in the Dodd-Frank financial reform bill of 2010. David has undertaken a most difficult and sensitive task. To explain and critique a statute that has been the subject of intense public and private debate, media attention, and voluminous congressional hearings, replete with congressional competition for primacy of jurisdiction, requires a high degree of courage and intelligence. David has exhibited both.

The process that resulted in the Dodd–Frank reform has the makings of at least three challenging documentaries or films. The threat of financial reform galvanized a broad base of opposition. The financial community, which ironically may be charged with having been a primary culprit in causing the financial crisis that almost dismembered the global financial system, generally was unalterably opposed to any meaningful financial reform. It mounted an extensive and extremely costly lobbying effort that enlisted the extensive cooperation of the House minority leader, Congressman John Boehner, who worked closely with the lobbyists in the attempt to defeat financial reform.

The New Financial Deal comprehensively and skillfully navigates the circumstances that created an environment for financial reform. The book illuminates the strains, pressures, and vicissitudes of attempting to enact a remedial statute that may materially affect the way business is conducted. The book describes the new world of finance that had evolved during the first decade of the twenty-first century that included new forms of investments and securities, such as derivatives, which were barely understood because of their esoteric and opaque characteristics. They befuddled regulators, to the extent they were regulated at all, and enabled huge risk taking. Also, access to credit enabled excessive leverage that put investors and the economy at great risk.

The crushing circumstances of the financial disaster are vividly described in *The New Financial Deal*. The crosscurrents that arose in respect of the need for financial reform and the scope of any financial reform are presented with clarity. *The New Financial Deal* properly raises the issue of whether the Dodd–Frank reform and its failure to deal with global concerns will result in real, meaningful financial reform that will prevent another financial crisis similar to that of 2008. The answer is not crystal clear, as *The New Financial Deal* illustrates.

The New Financial Deal is mandatory reading for all those interested in the financial markets and the global economy. David Skeel is to be commended for casting sunlight, the best disinfectant, on the events preceding the enactment of the Dodd–Frank reform, its efficacy, and the potential consequences, intended and unintended.

HARVEY R. MILLER
Lead Bankruptcy Attorney
for Lehman Brothers

Introduction

J
ust as surely as little boys on sleds follow a winter snowfall—to paraphrase the Yale economist Arthur Okun—a rip-roaring financial crisis is bound to result in a new swath of financial regulation.

Such, famously, was the case during the years following the stock market crash of 1929, when Congress passed—and President Franklin Roosevelt signed into law—a slew of financial reforms designed both to reduce the rampant speculation and risk taking that infected the nation's banking system and to increase the disclosure about companies seeking to sell their securities to public investors. The Securities Act of 1933 was the first federal law to regulate the sale of securities to investors, and required corporations to register their securities by filing a mountain of disclosure with the Securities and Exchange Commission (SEC), which was established the following year. (In the one-year interim period, the Federal Trade Commission approved the issuance of corporate securities.) The so-called 1933 Act required the SEC to approve an issuer's "registration statement" before the securities could be sold to investors. By and large for the past 77 years, the system has worked well and prevented most egregious scams.

There also was the Banking Act of 1933—more commonly known as the Glass-Steagall Act—that not only created the Federal Deposit Insurance Corporation but also forced banks to choose between commercial banking, which took deposits from the general public, and investment banking, which focused on the supposedly riskier activities of underwriting stocks and bonds. The Glass-Steagall Act gave banks until 1936 to make their decisions and was relatively straightforward: Choose one or the other, with the idea being that American savers would be protected from the tendency of bankers to take unwarranted risks with their money.

For most banks, this decision was simple, since few dabbled in both commercial and investment banking. Goldman Sachs, which to this day has little interaction with the public, stuck with investment banking, as did Lehman Brothers and Lazard Frères & Co. J.P. Morgan & Co., which had feet in both camps, chose commercial banking and jettisoned the investment-banking partners, who together formed Morgan Stanley & Co., which this year is celebrating its 75th anniversary. In 1932, the First Boston Corporation was founded as the investment banking arm (through the combination of a few firms) of the First National Bank of Boston; in 1934, per Glass-Steagall, First Boston was spun out of the commercial bank and became the first publicly traded Wall Street firm.

In the wake of Glass-Steagall, Wall Street seemed to mature, steady, and settle into a reliable pattern of behavior, none of which particularly threatened the stability of the financial system. By and large, the small, private partnerships that comprised Wall Street took prudent risks with their partners' money. Many thrived, and their partners got rich.

Not that Wall Street had stopped being a dangerous place. For instance, there was the—long forgotten now—back-office crisis of the late 1960s and early 1970s, which started during 1967 when trading volumes on the major stock exchanges exploded, and the poorly capitalized Wall Street partnerships were ill equipped to handle the extensive paperwork of settling trades occasioned by the sudden and unexpected upsurge in trading. Many firms were slow to add the back-office personnel required to handle the new flow. Unfortunately, when the personnel were eventually hired—in a rush, of course—talent suffered. Some firms were drowning in a sea of unprocessed, and inaccurately accounted for, paper.

But by the end of 1969, "the worst of the paperwork problems had been surmounted," according to Lee Arning, then a New York Stock Exchange executive. The crisis, though, had just begun, for at the very moment that many brokerages had increased their personnel costs to scale the mountain of paper, the volume of business fell off a cliff. There was a feeling that 1970 was capitalism's most acute test since 1929. "We were looking at the world from a 650 Dow Jones, the Penn Central bankruptcy, a credit crisis, Cambodia, Kent State—and we didn't know where anything was going and it was a pretty grim world at this time," Felix Rohatyn, one of the senior partners at Lazard Frères & Co., told the *New York Times*.

By midsummer 1970, Rohatyn had a full-fledged crisis to resolve as head of the New York Stock Exchange's Crisis Committee: The near dissolution of the old-line, blue-blood retail brokerage Hayden, Stone & Co., where Joseph P. Kennedy had begun to build the fortune that would be used to propel his second son to the presidency. (Joseph Kennedy was also the first chairman of the SEC.) Hayden, Stone had 62 offices nationwide, but its back-office systems were a mess. Compounding its problems, the firm's older partners, upon retiring, were withdrawing their capital from the firm. This, combined with the failing fortunes on Wall Street in general, created operating losses that together pushed Hayden, Stone dangerously close to default. Although Wall Street would be aghast, Rohatyn quickly found a savior for Hayden, Stone in Sandy Weill, the wunderkind financier who had presciently built a state-of-the-art securities clearing operation at his firm, Cogan, Berlind, Weill & Levitt (known as "Corned Beef with Lettuce" among Wall Street wags). Rohatyn decided that Weill, who would go on to create the financial behemoth Citigroup, was one of the few people able to grapple quickly with Hayden's accounting deficiencies. Rohatyn then proceeded to orchestrate a few more mergers, matching struggling brokers with their healthier brethren. Eventually, the crisis passed.

By the early 1990s, though, commercial banks—with J.P. Morgan, Citibank, and Chase Manhattan in the forefront—began encroaching on the turf of the investment banks, and sought to underwrite debt and equity securities and to provide mergers and acquisitions (M&A) advice. Commercial banks figured that, since they were taking the balance sheet risks by lending to corporate America, they might as well also get a slice of the lucrative fee-based business that Wall Street was hoovering up without seeming to take balance-sheet risk. In 1998, thanks to Sandy Weill, the Rasputin of finance, and his proposed merger between Travelers, which owned Salomon Smith Barney, and Citibank, the walls that separated commercial banking and investment banking came crashing down. In 1999, President Clinton signed the Gramm-Leach-Bliley Act, which made de jure what was already de facto: the Glass-Steagall Act was dead.

In the following decade, all hell broke loose. And the rest is history. Thanks to the financial crisis of 2007 and 2008, we have the Dodd-Frank Wall Street Reform and Consumer Protection Act, which President Obama signed into law in July 2010. Unlike the financial reform that emerged in the 1930s, which was fairly clear and explicit about what compliance meant for Wall Street, the Dodd-Frank Act's 2,300 pages seem to have muddied the already choppy waters: Must banks dump their proprietary traders? Can they still own hedge funds? What about private equity funds? Are banks actually limited to having just 3 percent of their Tier 1 capital invested in alternative investments? What types of derivatives will end up being traded on an exchange? How many clearinghouses will there be? The answers to these questions—and many others—must await the laborious process of drafting new regulations by the SEC, the Treasury, and the Federal Reserve, among others, as required by the new law.

While we wait and wonder what the true denouement of the Dodd-Frank Act will be, we are blessed with Professor David Skeel's timely, informative, and lucid explanation of the ins and outs of the new law. For readers trying to understand what Dodd-Frank will likely mean for Wall Street's future—and for ours—Skeel skillfully dissects the Act's nuances and intricacies and provides regulators a road map for how to make sure Wall Street doesn't double-cross us again anytime soon.

WILLIAM D. COHAN
Author of *House of Cards*, *The Last Tycoons*,
and an upcoming title on Goldman Sachs
to be published in 2011

A Few Major Characters

Ben Bernanke: Chairman, Federal Reserve, 2006–

Ben Bernanke had been a longtime economics professor at Princeton University when he was nominated to be a Governor of the Federal Reserve in 2002. As a scholar, he was best known for his studies of the causes of the Great Depression. Bernanke has often vowed not to repeat the Depression-era Fed's mistake of restricting access to funds during a crisis. Whatever one thinks of Bernanke's performance, there is no doubt that Bernanke and his fellow Federal Reserve Governors made good on his vow, steering funds to Bear Stearns, American International Group (AIG), the commercial paper market, and other recipients. He, Henry Paulson, and Timothy Geithner were the three musketeers of the regulatory response to the Panic of 2008.

Christopher Dodd

A three-term senator from Connecticut, Christopher Dodd announced in late 2009 that he would not be running for reelection in 2010.

Dodd's decision not to run was construed by many as a response both to a minor scandal—he had been given a below-market home loan by Countrywide Financial, the leading subprime lender—and to the dimming electoral prospects for congressional Democrats. As chair of the Senate Banking Committee, Dodd was the point person for the legislation in the Senate. Dodd was critical of some of the populist additions to the Act, such as the Volcker Rule.

Barney Frank

A longtime member of Congress from Massachusetts and chair of the House Financial Services Committee, Barney Frank was the point person for the legislation in the House. Frank was criticized during the Panic of 2008 for having resisted reform of Fannie Mae and Freddie Mac earlier in the decade. Frank was a strong advocate of the new Consumer Financial Protection Bureau and the more populist additions to the Act.

Richard Fuld: Chief Executive Officer, Lehman Brothers, 1994–2008

Richard Fuld was seen as something of a Lehman hero early in the decade, having risen through the ranks in a long career at the bank. His reputation quickly changed after the fateful summer of 2008, when Lehman failed to reach a deal with any of several possible buyers and investors, and then collapsed in September.

Timothy Geithner: Secretary of the Treasury, 2009–

The son of a diplomat, Tim Geithner has often been described as a former Wall Street banker, but he never actually worked in the private sector on Wall Street. After a short stint in Henry Kissinger's consulting firm, Geithner worked in the Treasury Department during the Clinton administration in the 1990s. This period saw bailouts of Mexico in

1994–1995 and (with funding from Wall Street banks) the hedge fund Long-Term Capital Management in 1998. As president of the New York Federal Reserve Bank, a position he held from 2003 to 2009, Geithner joined Henry Paulson and Ben Bernanke as the key architects of the bailouts of 2008. He and Larry Summers were the most important Obama administration advisers on the Dodd-Frank Act.

Henry Paulson: Secretary of the Treasury, 2006–2009

Henry Paulson was the head of the investment bank Goldman Sachs, after a long career as a investment banker at Goldman, when he joined the Bush administration as secretary of the Treasury in 2006. Paulson initially declined consideration, but then agreed to take the post on the condition that he have regular access to the President. He appears to have favored the Bear Stearns and AIG bailouts, and to have argued against a bailout of Lehman to send a signal that no company could count on receiving a bailout. He later claimed that the government did not have the power to bail out Lehman, because Lehman did not have adequate collateral to secure a loan under the Federal Reserve's emergency lending powers. He asked Congress for the funding that became the $700 billion Troubled Asset Relief Program (TARP) legislation in October 2008, and spearheaded the use of $17 billion of the money for loans to General Motors and Chrysler.

Lawrence Summers: Director, National Economic Council, 2009–2010

The son of two economists and the nephew of two others (Nobel Prize winners Paul Samuelson and Kenneth Arrow), Larry Summers was a wunderkind who earned tenure at Harvard University at the age of 28. He served as assistant secretary of the Treasury under Robert Rubin, then took over as Treasury secretary at the end of the Clinton administration. Summers became president of Harvard in 2001, but his tenure turned rocky after he suggested at a conference that scientists should study the possibility that there are more intelligent men than women "at the high end." One year and several more controversies later, he was forced to step down. Summers crept back into the public eye in a more favorable way as a result of a series of columns he wrote on economic issues for the *Financial Times* in 2007 and 2008. He was an important adviser to Barack Obama during Obama's presidential campaign. Many observers suspect that Obama would have nominated him as Treasury secretary if it weren't for the controversies at Harvard. In his post as director of the National Economic Council, which did not require Senate confirmation, Summers has been a key adviser to President Obama. He and Geithner appear to have significantly shaped the administration's contributions to the Dodd-Frank Act.

Paul Volcker

Paul Volcker is revered by many in Washington and elsewhere for his tough-minded handling of the rampant inflation of the late 1970s. As chair of the Federal Reserve, he and his fellow Federal Reserve Governors ratcheted up interest rates. Although some believe that the Fed stance cost President Carter reelection, it is widely viewed as having tamed inflation. During the 2008 campaign, Volcker was an important adviser to Barack Obama. But his role sharply diminished after the election. Volcker's signature position during the debates on the Dodd-Frank Act was a proposal that commercial banks be banned from engaging in proprietary trading—trading in derivatives and other financial instruments for their own accounts. The administration initially was cool to the proposal, but President Obama endorsed it—calling it the Volcker Rule—two days after the election of Scott Brown to Senator Edward Kennedy's seat in Massachusetts suggested that populist discontent with health care reform and the bailouts of 2008 was widespread.

Elizabeth Warren

A law professor at Harvard, Elizabeth Warren is a longtime critic of the credit card industry and advocate of the interests of consumer debtors.

Prior to the recent crisis, Warren was best known as the co-author of two books based on extensive empirical studies of consumer debtors, as well as *The Two-Income Trap*. Written with Warren's daughter, *The Two-Income Trap* argues that the two-income families that emerged after women began entering the workforce in large numbers in the 1970s are actually more economically vulnerable than their predecessors, not less. In late 2008, Warren was named by Senator Harry Reid to serve as chair of the TARP Oversight Committee, which has issued regular reports on monitoring expenditures under the TARP legislation that gave Treasury $700 billion to quell the crisis in the banking system. The proposal for a new consumer regulator was conceived by Warren, and outlined in articles she wrote in 2007 and 2008. Although Warren was the obvious choice to head the Consumer Financial Protection Bureau, it was unclear whether she could be confirmed over the opposition of Republicans and some moderate Democrats. To sidestep this impediment, President Obama named her as his assistant and as a special adviser to Treasury Secretary Geithner—and thus as de facto initial head—for the new Consumer Bureau.

Chapter 1

The Corporatist Turn
in American Regulation

W hen President Obama signed the Dodd–Frank Act into law on July 21, 2010, he began a new epoch in financial regulation. The old epoch dated back to the early 1930s, when President Roosevelt and the New Deal Congress enacted the securities acts of 1933 and 1934, as well as banking reforms that broke up the giant Wall Street banks and put deposit insurance in place for the first time. Never again, they promised, would investors be forced to live by their critical wits in unregulated markets, or ordinary Americans lose their life savings if their bank failed.

The new legislation comes in the third year of the worst American financial crisis since the Great Depression, a crisis that was exacerbated by financial instruments and new forms of financing that were not dreamed of in that earlier era. Most Americans had never even heard of the financial assembly line known as securitization before the collapse of major mortgage lenders like Countrywide and the more cataclysmic failures of Bear Stearns, Fannie Mae, Freddie Mac, Lehman Brothers, and American International Group (AIG). Many still don't understand just what this process is all about—other than to repeat familiar clichés about the "slicing and dicing" of mortgages—but they know that the failure to adequately regulate these innovations has figured prominently in the crisis.

After watching the government bail out Bear Stearns and AIG in 2008, and pump well over $100 billion into Citigroup, Bank of America, and the other big banks the same year, Americans also know that the existing regulatory framework could not adequately oversee our largest financial institutions. Perhaps the best evidence of just how rickety that old regulatory structure was can be found in the best-selling books about the financial crisis. Bill Cohan's *House of Cards* showed just how little the nation's top regulators—then-Treasury Secretary Henry Paulson, Federal Reserve Chair Ben Bernanke, and then-head of the New York Federal Reserve Bank Timothy Geithner—knew about Bear Stearns's financial condition as they decided the investment bank's fate. Andrew Ross Sorkin's riveting page-turner on the crisis, *Too Big to Fail*, revealed just how unscripted and unnervingly ad hoc the decisions whether to nationalize (as with Fannie Mae and Freddie Mac), let go (as with Lehman Brothers), or bail out (as with AIG) were in the calamitous months that followed. The picture of one page from Henry Paulson's phone log in Sorkin's book is enough to make one's heart stop.[1]

The Dodd-Frank Wall Street Reform and Consumer Protection Act—the Dodd-Frank Act for short—is the response to Americans' call for help, for a new regulatory framework for the twenty-first century. To understand what American financial life is likely to look like in 5, 10, or 20 years, and how regulators may respond to the next crisis, we need to understand the Dodd-Frank Act: both what it says and what it means. This, in a nutshell, is what the book you are reading is about.

The Path to Enactment

The Dodd-Frank Act got its start in March 2009, when the Department of the Treasury released a framework it called "Rules for the Regulatory Road" shortly before a major meeting of the G-20 nations. Treasury released a more complete White Paper and proposed legislative language several months later. The White Paper would provide the template for all of the major parts of the legislation that eventually passed.

Throughout the summer and fall of 2009, Treasury Secretary Tim Geithner and other defenders of the proposed legislation were hammered by critics. On the right, the emerging Tea Party movement lumped the financial reforms together with the health care legislation as evidence of the Big Government inclinations of the Obama administration, and condemned the reforms as institutionalizing the bailout policies of 2008. Many on the left were equally critical. For liberal critics, the bailouts and the proposed legislation suggested that the administration was catering to Wall Street, while doing very little to ease the suffering that the financial crisis had brought to Main Street.

In response to these criticisms, the administration tightened up portions of the legislation that could be construed as inviting bailouts. They also insisted that the legislation wouldn't perpetuate the bailouts of the prior year. By giving regulators the power to dismantle systemically important financial institutions that were on the brink of collapse, they argued, it actually would end the use of bailouts.

The next major step toward enactment came when Congressman Barney Frank steered a version of the proposed legislation through his Financial Services Committee, and then, on December 11, 2009, through the House of Representatives.

In January 2009, the Obama administration was forced to make a major concession to populist criticism of the legislation by the stunning victory of Republican Scott Brown in the election to fill Edward Kennedy's Senate seat in Massachusetts. Two days after Brown's election, President Obama endorsed a proposal by former Federal Reserve Chairman Paul Volcker that would ban banks from engaging in proprietary trading—that is, trading for their own accounts. Until the

Brown election, the administration had resisted the proposal as an undesirable interference with the activities of the big banks.

Even after this shift, the fate of the legislation remained uncertain for several months. Given the heavy Democratic majorities in Congress and the obvious inadequacies of existing regulation, most observers thought some version of the legislation would pass. But it wasn't clear what version, or when.

The pivotal push once again came from outside the halls of Congress. On April 19, the Securities and Exchange Commission (SEC) sued Goldman Sachs, which had emerged as a principal villain of the financial crisis—"a great vampire squid wrapped around the face of humanity, relentlessly jamming its blood funnel into anything that smells like money," in the immortal words of *Rolling Stone* magazine. Approved by a 3 to 2 vote of the SEC's commissioners, the SEC lawsuit alleged that Goldman had defrauded investors by failing to tell them that the mortgage-related investments it had sold them were picked in part by a hedge fund that was betting that the mortgages would default. The securities fraud allegations transformed the political landscape, shifting the momentum decisively in favor of the legislation. On May 20, the Senate passed its version, known as the Dodd Bill after Senate Banking Committee Chair Christopher Dodd. In the ensuing two months, a conference committee worked out the differences between the two bills, and with the President's signature, Dodd-Frank was born.[2]

The Two Goals of the Dodd-Frank Act

Contrary to rumors that the Dodd-Frank Act is an incoherent mess, the Wall Street Reform portion of its 2,319 pages (a mere 800 or so when the margins and spacing have been squeezed) has two very clear objectives. Its first objective is to limit the risk of contemporary finance—what critics often call the shadow banking system; and the second is to limit the damage caused by the failure of a large financial institution. (Although the Wall Street reforms are this book's particular focus, it also devotes a chapter to the new consumer regulator, which is the heart of Dodd-Frank's contribution to consumer protection.)

The Dodd-Frank Act tackles the first task by putting brand-new regulatory structures in place for both the *instruments* and the *institutions* of the new financial world. The principal instruments in question are derivatives. A derivative is simply a contract between two parties (each called a counterparty), whose value is based on changes in an interest rate, currency, or almost anything else, or on the occurrence of some specified event (such as a company's default). An airline may buy an oil derivative—a contract under which it will be paid if the price of oil has risen at the end of the contract term—to hedge against changes in oil prices. Southwest Airline's judicious use of these derivatives was one of the keys to its early success.

The Dodd-Frank Act's main strategy for managing the riskiness of these contracts is to require that derivatives be cleared and traded on exchanges. To clear a derivative (or anything else, for that matter), the parties arrange for a clearinghouse to backstop both parties' performance on the contract. If the bank that had sold Southwest an oil derivative failed, for instance, the clearinghouse would pay Southwest the difference between the current and original oil price or would arrange for a substitute contract. If the same derivative were exchange traded, it would have standardized terms and would be purchased on an organized exchange, rather than negotiated privately by Southwest and the bank. Clearing reduces the risk to each of the parties directly, while exchange trading reduces risk to them and to the financial system indirectly by making the derivatives market more transparent.

To better regulate institutions, the Dodd-Frank Act seeks to single out the financial institutions that are most likely to cause systemwide problems if they fail, and subjects them to more intensive regulation. The legislation focuses in particular on bank holding companies that have at least $50 billion in assets, and nonbank financial institutions such as investment banks or insurance holding companies that a new Financial Stability Oversight Council deems to be systemically important. ("Bank" in this context means a commercial bank—a bank that accepts customer deposits. A bank holding company is a group of affiliated companies that has at least one commercial bank somewhere in the network, or has chosen to be subject to banking regulation, as Goldman Sachs and Morgan Stanley did in the fall of 2008. I will sometimes use "bank" to refer to either.) Banks like Citigroup or Bank of America automatically qualify, as do 34 others, whereas an insurance company like AIG will be included only if the Council identifies it as systemically important. The Dodd-Frank Act instructs regulators to require that these systemically important firms keep a larger buffer of capital than ordinary financial institutions, to reduce the danger that they will fail.[3]

If Dodd-Frank's first objective is to limit risk before the fact—before an institution or market collapses—the second objective is to limit the destruction caused in the event that a systemically important institution does indeed fail, despite everyone's best efforts to prevent that from happening. For this second objective, the legislation introduces a new insolvency framework—the Dodd-Frank resolution rules. If regulators find that a systemically important financial institution has defaulted or is in danger of default, they can file a petition in federal court in Washington, D.C., commencing resolution proceedings, and appoint the Federal Deposit Insurance Corporation (FDIC) as receiver to take over the financial institution and liquidate it, much as the FDIC has long done with ordinary commercial banks.

Like the New Deal reforms, which gave us the FDIC and the SEC, among others, the Dodd-Frank Act creates several new regulators to achieve these two objectives, including the Financial Stability Oversight Council, whose members include the heads of all the major financial regulators, and a new federal insurance regulator. I have already mentioned that the other major new regulator (the Consumer Financial Protection Bureau) will also come into our story, in part as a foil to the key Wall Street banks.

A Brief Tour of Other Reforms

Throughout, the book focuses primarily on the reforms that relate most directly to the two goals just described. Although these are the most important of the reforms, several others have received significant attention. I give each at least glancing comment elsewhere in the book, but it may be useful to identify them briefly and more explicitly here.

The first two are a pair of corporate governance reforms, each of which is designed to give shareholders more authority. The more important of the two is a provision that simply gives the SEC the power to require a company to include shareholder nominees for director along with the company's own nominees when it sends proxy materials to all of its shareholders before its annual meeting. The SEC has already taken advantage of this authority, approving a regulation that will allow shareholders with at least 3 percent of a corporation's stock to include nominees for up to 25 percent of the directorial positions. The second, which was one of President Obama's campaign promises, will require that shareholders be given a nonbinding vote on the compensation packages of the company's directors and top executives. Neither is likely to have a particularly large effect, although the first—known as proxy access—has generated anxiety in directorial circles. These critics complain that unions and pensions will use the new shareholder power to promote their own agendas.[4]

The Dodd-Frank Act also took aim at a few of the problems plaguing the credit rating industry. The credit rating agencies—Standard & Poor's, Moody's Investors Service, and Fitch—did a notoriously poor job with the mortgage-related securities at the heart of the subprime crisis, handing out investment grade ratings to many securities that later defaulted. One problem with the current system is that the bank whose securities are being rated pays for the rating. (As my students like to say, it's as if a school used a grading system in which students paid for their grades.) Although the legislation did not eliminate the "issuer pays" feature of credit ratings, it requires financial regulators to change the many rules that require entities like pension funds and insurance companies to buy securities that are certified as investment grade by a credit rating agency. These changes, it is hoped, will diminish the pressure to rely on credit rating agencies. Removal of the artificial demand for credit rated securities could indeed significantly improve the credit rating process. Dodd-Frank also includes a variety of new rules for the governance of a rating agency.[5]

Finally, the legislation requires hedge funds to register for the first time. In the past, the defining characteristic of hedge funds was their exclusion from securities laws and related regulation that would otherwise require disclosure and oversight. Under the Dodd-Frank Act, hedge fund advisers must now register and make themselves available for periodic inspections.[6]

Each of these new provisions is related to the two principal objectives of the Act, but each is more at the periphery than the center. The core is Dodd-Frank's treatment of derivatives, its regulation of systemically important financial institutions, and its new rules for resolving their financial distress, together with the counterweight of the Consumer Financial Protection Bureau.

Two Themes That Emerge

I wish I could say that the new regulatory regime will be as successful as the New Deal legislation it is designed to update. But I fear it won't be. Unless its most dangerous features are arrested, the legislation could permanently ensconce the worst tendencies of the regulatory interventions during the recent crisis as long-term regulatory policy.

The problem isn't with Dodd-Frank's two objectives. The objectives are right on target. The problem is with how they are handled. The two themes that emerge, repeatedly and unmistakably, from the 2,000 pages of legislation are (1) government partnership with the largest financial institutions and (2) ad hoc intervention by regulators rather than a more predictable, rules-based response to crises. Each could dangerously distort American finance, making it more politically charged, less vibrant, and further removed from basic rule-of-law principles than ever before in modern American financial history.

The first theme, as I just noted, is government partnership with the largest Wall Street banks and financial institutions. Dodd-Frank singles out a group of financial institutions for special treatment. The banks that meet the $50 billion threshold, and the nonbank financial institutions designated by the new Financial Stability Oversight Council as systemically important will be put in their own separate category.

Unlike in the New Deal, there is no serious effort to break the largest of these banks up or to meaningfully scale them down. Because they are special, and because no one really believes the largest will be allowed to fail, they will have a competitive advantage over other financial institutions. They will be able to borrow money more cheaply, for instance, than banks that are not in the club. Dodd-Frank also gives regulators a variety of mechanisms they can use to channel political policy through the dominant institutions. The partnership works in both directions: special treatment for the Wall Street giants, new political policy levers for the government.

The second theme overlaps with the first: Dodd-Frank enshrines a system of ad hoc interventions by regulators that are divorced from basic rule-of-law constraints. The unconstrained regulatory discretion reaches its zenith with the new resolution rules for financial institutions in distress. Dodd-Frank resolution is designed for systemically important financial institutions that have been singled out for special treatment. But the rules do not even require that an institution be designated as systemically important in advance. If regulators want to take over a struggling bank, they can simply do so as long as they can say with a straight face that it is "in default or in danger of default" and its default could have "serious adverse effects" on stability. Not only this, but they may be able to take over every affiliate in the bank's network. Once the institution is in government hands, the FDIC can pick and choose among creditors, deciding to pay some in full while leaving the rest with the dregs that remain after the favored creditors are paid.

The basic expectations of the rule of law—that the rules will be transparent and knowable in advance, that important issues will not be left to the whim of regulators—are subverted by this framework. Nor is the tendency limited to the end-of-life issues I have been discussing. The Dodd-Frank Act invites ad hoc intervention with healthy financial institutions as well.

The two tendencies I have just described will not come as a surprise to anyone who followed the legislative debates that led to the Dodd-Frank Act. Massachusetts Institute of Technology (MIT) Professor Simon Johnson and Nobel Prize economist Joseph Stiglitz, among others, insisted that the largest banks need to be broken up because they are too big to effectively regulate and because they distort the financial markets. I will refer to this perspective throughout the book as Brandeisian, in honor of Louis Brandeis, the Roosevelt adviser and Supreme Court justice, who advocated this view throughout the early twentieth century.[7]

Similarly, many critics complained about the dangers of the new legislation's casual disregard of the rule of law during the legislative debates. The contrast between the new resolution rules and the more predictable, transparent, rule-oriented bankruptcy process was a frequent subject of concern.

The administration and advocates of the legislation did not simply ignore these criticisms. At several points, they were forced to make concessions. The most important concession is the provision now known as the Volcker Rule. Promoted by Paul Volcker, the popular former chairman of the Federal Reserve and an adviser to President Obama during the 2008 election campaign, the Volcker Rule is a throwback to New Deal legislation that made it illegal to conduct commercial and investment banking under the same umbrella. As noted earlier, the Volcker rule prohibits commercial banks from engaging in proprietary trading—that is, trading and speculating for the bank's own account—which is central to contemporary investment banking, and limits their investment in hedge funds or equity funds.

Responding to criticisms that the legislation would invite a repeat of the ad hoc bailouts of 2008, proponents of the legislation tinkered with the resolution rules. This second set of concessions amended the emergency lending authority that the Federal Reserve used to fund the bailouts, transplanted several bankruptcy provisions into the Dodd-Frank resolution framework, and added a requirement that the institutions subject to the regime be liquidated.

In theory, these concessions could give regulators the ability to rein in the giant financial institutions. But, in a classic illustration of the law of unintended consequences, both are more likely to make the prevailing tendencies of the new legislation worse. Although the Volcker Rule is forcing banks to adjust their operations, the concept of proprietary trading is so slippery that its application will depend on how, and how strictly, regulators interpret it. This will entail an ongoing negotiation

between the largest banks and the regulators, which could simply reinforce the partnership between the two, with the government softening
its definition of proprietary in return for an implicit agreement by the
banks not to shift their proprietary trading operations overseas.

The adjustments that purport to end bailouts and ad hoc interventions will do nothing of the kind. Although the restrictions on the
Federal Reserve's emergency lending authority are based on a valuable
principle—that the Fed should not single out individual firms for
rescue—they will not prevent future bailouts. Regulators can pressure other systemically important firms to fund a bailout—as they
did when the Long-Term Capital Management hedge fund collapsed
in 1998—or they can simply maneuver around the restrictions by
creating an across-the-board lending facility that is really a single firm
bailout in disguise. If regulators do take over a large financial institution under their resolution authority, they can evade the bankruptcy-
like provisions by simply agreeing to pay favored creditors in full under
the FDIC's carte blanche to cherry-pick among creditors.

The two central themes of the Dodd-Frank Act—government partnership with the largest financial institutions and ad hoc intervention—
survived the Brandeisian concessions fully intact.

Fannie Mae Effect

I have made several references already to the possibility that the
government will channel political policy through the large financial
institutions that are singled out for special treatment. Historically, this
kind of collaboration between the government and large businesses has
been called corporatism. It is a familiar feature of corporate and financial
regulation in Europe. Perhaps I should be more specific about how this
could work in the Dodd-Frank Act.

Most pervasively, the Dodd-Frank Act invites the government to
channel political policy through the big financial institutions by giving regulators sweeping discretion in the enforcement of nearly every
aspect of the legislation. Suppose, for instance, that regulators are
determining whether a group of Citigroup bankers are engaged in

proprietary trading at a time when the government is unhappy with the big oil companies, or with weapons manufacturers. It is not hard to imagine Citigroup's directors concluding that they had better limit the bank's financing of the disfavored industry if they wish to get sympathetic treatment as regulators decide whether the bank is in compliance with the Volcker Rule. Many other provisions will give regulators similar leverage in their partnership with the largest financial institutions.

This, of course, was how Fannie Mae and Freddie Mac functioned under both Republican and Democratic administrations before the two entities collapsed and were nationalized in 2008.[8]

The corporatist dimension of the legislation is further evident in the extraordinary authority the Dodd-Frank Act gives to the secretary of the Treasury and the Treasury Department. Because the Treasury secretary is directly responsible to the President, he is the least independent, and the most political, of the financial regulators. Yet the Treasury secretary is given leadership responsibility on the new Financial Stability Oversight Council and in other areas. Dodd-Frank also locates an enormous new research facility—the Office of Financial Research—in the Treasury Department. Control over knowledge is power, of course, which suggests that the ostensibly neutral research facility could become yet another channel of Treasury influence.

Covering Their Tracks

The special treatment of the largest firms and the reliance on ad hoc intervention raises a perplexing puzzle. Given that this is precisely what so many Americans found offensive about the bailouts of 2008 and were so anxious to reform, how did we end up with legislation that has such similar qualities?

Perhaps the moral is that bank-government partnership and ad hoc intervention in a crisis are simply unavoidable. We cannot dismiss this possibility out of hand. In a different context—national security— several top legal scholars have argued that in times of national crisis, the executive branch of our government will inevitably take unilateral action, without waiting for Congress. The executive branch, they argue, is more responsive to the concerns of the country as a whole, and is better able to act quickly and decisively.[9]

Perhaps financial crises are similar. The rule of law will always give way in a crisis. But even if it is impossible to guarantee that there will never be another ad hoc bailout, this reasoning doesn't really explain Dodd-Frank itself. It doesn't explain why the legislation protects the largest Wall Street banks, and it doesn't explain why the legislation encourages ad hoc intervention, in good times as well as crises, rather than trying to make it as rare as possible.

A different explanation is much more plausible: The Dodd-Frank Act was an opportunity for the same regulators that gave us the Bear Stearns and AIG bailouts to cover their tracks. The legislation was drafted by the same people who designed the bailout strategy, and it shows.

When future generations look back on the origins of the Dodd-Frank Act, this fact may seem more amazing than any other. Consider a simple analogy. Every bank has two different departments for the loans it makes to businesses. In one department, loan officers make the loans. But if the borrower falls into financial distress, the loan is transferred to another department, the workout group. Banks do not let the original loan officer handle the negotiations to restructure the loan, because they suspect the loan officer's judgment would be clouded by the rationales that caused the loan officer to make the loan at the beginning. Banks know, and have known for generations, that they need a fresh set of eyes after things go wrong.

Dodd-Frank ignored this basic principle of sound business; it never had that fresh set of eyes. As I have mentioned, the main architects of the 2008 bailouts were then–Treasury Secretary Henry Paulson, then-head of the New York Fed Timothy Geithner, and Federal Reserve Chair Ben Bernanke. Of the three, Geithner seems to have the deepest commitment to ad hoc bailouts and to financial policy as a friendly negotiation between elite regulators and the heads of the largest banks. (Geithner's coziness with the dominant banks explains why he has often been mistakenly identified as a former Goldman Sachs banker.) By bringing Geithner into his administration as Treasury secretary, President Obama ensured that the earlier policies would be carried into the new administration. Ben Bernanke still holds the same post he occupied throughout the crisis, chair of the Federal Reserve. Of the three, only Paulson did not have a substantial role in framing the new financial legislation, although he did offer his own form of encouragement: a memoir recounting the bailouts through a revisionist lens, suggesting that all he, Bernanke, and Geithner had needed were more regulatory powers.[10]

Geithner's Treasury Department devised a framework that attempts to perfect what he, Paulson, and Bernanke did in 2008. By implication, the new law legitimates their bailouts and covers their tracks.

Is There Anything to Like?

A leading banking authority recently wrote to me in an e-mail that the Dodd-Frank Act is the "worst piece of financial legislation" in his lifetime, and suggested that it is a disaster from first page to last. Is he correct? Does the legislation lack even the smallest worthwhile contributions?[11]

I am not quite so pessimistic. Although the overall pattern of the legislation is disturbing, a handful of its contributions could genuinely improve the regulatory landscape. The new framework for clearing derivatives and trading them on exchanges is an unequivocal advance. To be sure, there are substantial uncertainties even here. The extent to which clearing and exchange trading will transform the derivatives markets for the better will depend, like much of Dodd-Frank, on how effectively the principal regulators implement the reforms—whether they ensure that most derivatives do in fact migrate to clearinghouses and exchanges, for instance, and how well they regulate the clearinghouses. But the reforms promise to make the derivatives markets far more transparent than in the past, and to diminish the risk that the default of a major financial institution will cause upheavals throughout the financial markets.

A second step forward is the new Consumer Financial Protection Bureau established by the legislation to serve as a consumer watchdog with respect to credit card and mortgage practices. Although the new bureau will be part of the Federal Reserve, it will be almost completely insulated from second-guessing by the Fed or other bank regulators. (Only if a regulation could cause a systemic crisis can other regulators override the Consumer Bureau.) Although some critics plausibly argue that the Consumer Bureau has been given too much power, consumers' interests were woefully underrepresented during the recent crisis. It never made sense to simply include consumer protection among the Fed's other tasks, for instance, since the Fed's primary concern is maintaining the stability of the banking system, which stands in considerable tension with consumer protection. Although consumer protection will still be within the Federal Reserve, it will be far more robust now that it is a separate operation.

I suspect my relative optimism may stem from another factor as well. The effects of government partnership with the largest financial institutions, and of the ad hoc framework for dealing with their financial distress, could not be more pernicious. We may see political factors influencing banking decisions, which could prevent promising but politically unconnected industries from getting the funding they need. We also may see another bailout the next time a systemically important financial institution or important company falls into distress. But I believe that some of the worst tendencies of the new legislation could be curbed with a few very simple reforms.

■ ■ ■

In the chapter that comprises Part I of the book—"Relearning the Financial Crisis"—I revisit two key events in the recent crisis. The first is the fall of Lehman. Rather than showing that bailouts are necessary and that bankruptcy does not work, as the conventional wisdom suggests, I argue that the problems caused by Lehman actually were the result of a regulatory bait-and-switch. With their earlier bailout of Bear Stearns, regulators had strongly signaled their intent to bail out any systemically important financial institution. But they pulled the rug out from under Lehman and its potential buyers by shifting course at the very last moment. The other key event whose significance has not been fully appreciated is the bailouts of Chrysler and General Motors. These bailouts were achieved first by appropriating funds meant for financial institutions and then by commandeering the bankruptcy process. The apparent success of those bailouts was construed by the regulators involved as a confirmation of the regulatory philosophy that underlies the Dodd–Frank Act.

The heart of the book comes in Part II, Chapters 3 through 8. After an inside account of the legislative process, drawing on my own trips back and forth to and from Washington, D.C., in Chapter 3, the chapters that follow carefully explore each of the major planks of the new regulatory framework, explaining what they will do, what they mean, and what some of their unintended consequences may be.

In the final part, I look to the future. The first chapter in Part III outlines several simple bankruptcy reforms that would curb the excesses of the new government-bank partnership and the reliance on ad hoc regulatory intervention; and the second considers ways to address international dimensions of the new financial order that are largely neglected by the Dodd–Frank Act.

Although much of the book is critical, I conclude on a note of hope.

Part I

RELEARNING THE FINANCIAL CRISIS

Chapter 2

The Lehman Myth

Every reform effort has a central narrative. In this chapter, we consider the standard narrative that shaped the new financial deal. As we will see, and as many readers already know, the very essence of the narrative can be summed up in two words: Lehman Brothers.

As I first wrote these words, former Treasury Secretary Henry Paulson had just given an interview for the *New York Times* praising the new legislation on the verge of its enactment. "'We would have loved to have something like this for Lehman Brothers. There's no doubt about it,'" Paulson said. He was referring, his interviewer noted, "to a provision of the bill known as resolution authority, which would enable the government to unwind a failing investment bank or insurance company in an orderly way without forcing it into bankruptcy, thus avoiding the unintended consequences that a bankruptcy might create."[1]

This chapter is an exercise in reprogramming that will call into question nearly every assumption in Paulson's comments. To understand what the new legislation means, we begin with the conventional wisdom about Lehman's collapse. We then can begin to construct a more accurate story about the financial failures of 2008 and their implications for financial regulation. This story will change two key words in the Lehman myth: In place of Lehman Brothers, I will put Bear Stearns.

If Bear Stearns had not been rescued earlier in 2008, the six months between its collapse and Lehman's would have looked very different. But the government committed itself to a pattern of ad hoc interventions that would continue throughout the crisis and into the architecture of the Dodd-Frank Act itself.

The final link in the chain from Bear Stearns to the new legislation was the Chrysler and General Motors bankruptcies of spring and summer 2009. All of the earlier bailouts had been carried out by the Bush administration. Although rescue funding began under Bush, Chrysler and GM belonged to Obama and his Auto Task Force, led by Treasury Secretary Tim Geithner and National Economic Council director Larry Summers. In addition to confirming the new administration's commitment to bailouts as the strategy of choice when an important company falls into financial distress, the carmaker bankruptcies pioneered a new kind of intervention. In these bailouts, the government not only rescued the companies, but also decided which of its creditors to pay and which to abandon. These are precisely the kinds of powers the government would assign itself under the new financial legislation.

I begin with the Lehman myth. After showing the flaws in the conventional wisdom that Lehman's bankruptcy triggered the worst of the financial crisis, I imagine how the crisis might have unfolded if Bear Stearns had not been rescued. I then turn to the carmakers, whose rescues completed the groundwork for the Dodd-Frank Act.

The Stock Narrative

Although there are variations, as with any good story, the Lehman myth generally goes something like this. Prior to the shock of Lehman's bankruptcy filing in the early-morning hours of September 15, 2008, the Panic of 2008 — then generally known as the subprime crisis — was

more or less manageable. Federal regulators had started off on the right
foot by bailing out Bear Stearns and midwifing its sale to JPMorgan
Chase in March 2008. They also were wise to bail out American
International Group (AIG) six months later, although they botched
the execution. Lehman was the one big exception—an exception
that showed once and for all that bankruptcy is not adequate to handle
the collapse of a major financial institution. The Lehman bankruptcy
unleashed a tidal wave of consequences that nearly brought down
the American economy, as well as many economies elsewhere in the
world. This, in condensed form, is the Lehman myth.[2]

Shorthand references to the Lehman myth by journalists and
experts alike have been ubiquitous in the two years since the bankruptcy filing. "The Lehman bankruptcy triggered a chain reaction that
ripped through the financial markets," Simon Johnson and James Kwak
write in their book on the crisis. "A vigorous government response
was necessary," they continue, "particularly after the Lehman bankruptcy." "The government-sanctioned bankruptcy of a Wall Street firm
founded before the Civil War marked a new phase in the Great Panic,"
according to *Wall Street Journal* reporter David Wessel, "a moment
when financial markets went from bad to awful. The *Wall Street Journal*
dubbed it the 'Weekend That Wall Street Died.'"[3]

The more careful accounts, including the two just quoted, also give
additional details, starting with the effect of Lehman's default on its commercial paper—the short-term IOUs that are an important source of
financing for many companies. As is often the case, much of Lehman's
commercial paper was held by money market funds, which see commercial paper as a safe, attractive way to earn interest income. The largest
holder of Lehman's commercial paper—a fund called the Reserve Fund—
was forced to "break the buck"; that is, it was unable to guarantee its
investors that they would receive at least a dollar for every dollar they had
invested. This is a no-no in the money market business, and completely
spooked both the commercial paper market and money market funds.
The counterparties to Lehman's derivatives and other parties that had
contracts with Lehman also panicked, fearing that they would suffer
huge losses due to the bankruptcy filing. And the collapse triggered a
climate of fear in every corner of the financial markets, according to this

more detailed version of the conventional wisdom, even among market participants who did not have any direct exposure to Lehman. All of the turmoil that followed, the story continues—the rescue of AIG, the desperate appeal by Henry Paulson and Ben Bernanke for $700 billion of Troubled Asset Relief Program (TARP) funds, and everything else—can be traced to the Lehman bankruptcy. Lehman's bankruptcy unleashed the panic, according to this reasoning, and bankruptcy invariably means a disorderly response to a financial institution's distress.

The three musketeers of the financial crisis—Paulson, Geithner, and Bernanke—have sought to solidify and subtly reshape the conventional wisdom. In their telling, the Lehman bankruptcy was a disaster but their hands were collectively tied. Because the Federal Reserve is authorized to provide rescue funding only if the recipient can put up good collateral to secure repayment, and because Lehman had very little usable collateral, they claim, the government could not legally bail Lehman out. Henry Paulson has been especially persistent in pressing this explanation. In his memoir of the crisis, for instance, he reports that "an evaluation of Lehman's assets had revealed a gaping hole in its balance sheet. The Fed could not legally lend to fill a hole in Lehman's capital. That was why we needed a buyer." This claim has been met with widespread and justifiable skepticism. The three didn't hesitate to stretch the law when they bailed out Bear Stearns and AIG; they clearly could have done the same if they had resolved to rescue Lehman.[4]

While the regulators' claim that they didn't have any choice hasn't proven especially persuasive, it has further entrenched the conventional wisdom about the consequences of Lehman's bankruptcy. Skeptics of the claim that regulators could not have bailed Lehman out often agree that bankruptcy for Lehman was a disaster.

The problem with this stock narrative is that it is almost completely wrong. It is wrong in suggesting that Lehman's collapse was the sole cause of the crisis. And it is wrong in its suggestion that bankruptcy inevitably means a disorderly failure. Lehman is an important part of a more accurate story, to be sure. And a few of the factual details are accurate if taken in isolation. It is the causal claims that are wildly misleading.

Lehman in Context

Even if we focus solely on the period right around the time of Lehman's bankruptcy filing, the claim that Lehman was the cause of the crisis does not withstand scrutiny. If Lehman single-handedly triggered crisis, we would expect to see a dramatic market reaction to Lehman's bankruptcy filing, and a much more muted response to the AIG bailout a bit less than two full days later. But this is not what the evidence shows.

Table 2.1 documents changes in several major indexes that occurred the day after the Lehman bankruptcy filing was announced, compared with the day following the AIG rescue loan.[5]

Looking across the four indexes, the daily market reactions surrounding the news of the Lehman bankruptcy filing and the AIG rescue loan indicate that the reaction to the AIG news was of equal, if not greater, magnitude. The fall in the stock market, as measured by the S&P 500 index, was virtually identical. The VIX, an index used to measure volatility (and informally known as the "fear index"), saw a slightly higher percentage increase following the Lehman bankruptcy. The TED spread, an indicator of credit market risk, saw a larger percentage point increase following the AIG bailout. (The TED spread is the difference between the three-month London Interbank Offered Rate [LIBOR]—an interest rate at which banks lend to each other—and the three-month U.S. Treasury bill rate.) Similarly, yields on

Table 2.1 Reactions to Lehman Bankruptcy and AIG Bailout

Index	Lehman			AIG		
	Sept. 12	Sept. 15	Change	Sept. 16	Sept. 17	Change
S&P 500	1,251.7	1,192.7	−4.71%	1,213.6	1,156.39	−4.71%
Volatility (VIX)	25.66	31.7	23.54%	30.3	36.22	19.54%
TED spread	1.35	2.01	0.66	2.19	3.02	0.84
13-week						
Treasury bill	1.46	0.81	−0.65	0.86	0.02	−0.84

Source: Ayotte and Skeel, 2010.

short-term U.S. Treasury bills (a measure of investors' flight to safe assets) fell more following the AIG news.

These indexes suggest, at a minimum, that the widespread belief that the Lehman Chapter 11 filing was the singular cause of the collapse in credit that followed is greatly overstated. The comparison also highlights that news of a major event can convey two distinct pieces of news at the same time: first, that a large, important entity is severely distressed and illiquid; and second, that a particular procedure was triggered to address it. In Lehman, the procedure was bankruptcy, while in AIG, the procedure was a rescue loan. The indicators in the table suggest that the market did not distinguish between the two distress resolution procedures; it focused instead on the implications of the distress itself.

Looking at a wider time frame, and from a slightly different perspective, John Taylor, a prominent economist and former undersecretary of the Treasury, presents further evidence that the Lehman myth seriously misconstrues the effects of Lehman's bankruptcy filing. Taylor looks first at the spread between the LIBOR rate for comparatively longer-term bank loans and the interest rate for overnight loans (overnight indexed swap [OIS] rate). The LIBOR-OIS spread is another key indicator of stress in the market, with the spread rising in the event of market turmoil.[6]

Over the course of 2008, the LIBOR-OIS spread fluctuated up and down within a roughly 50 to 100 basis points (0.5 to 1.0 percent) range. As reflected in Figure 2.1, on September 15, when Lehman filed for bankruptcy, it did rise a bit. It then dropped back down on September 16 before rising the following week. But none of these movements were dramatically out of line with its fluctuations throughout the year. The real jump, and the evidence of a real ratcheting up of the crisis, began with the announcement that the Fed and Treasury would be asking for $700 billion in TARP funds to respond to the crisis. From Friday, September 19, when the request was first announced, to September 23, when Paulson and Bernanke testified to Congress that $700 billion was needed to forestall a possible collapse of the market, the spread surged upward. It finally peaked at 350 basis points (3.5 percent) on October 13, when Paulson announced his plan to use TARP funds to purchase equity in troubled banks.

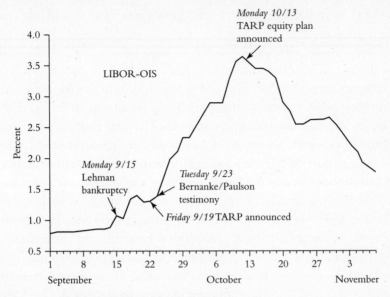

Figure 2.1   LIBOR-OIS Reaction to Fall 2008 Crisis
SOURCE: Hoover Institution Press. All Rights Reserved.

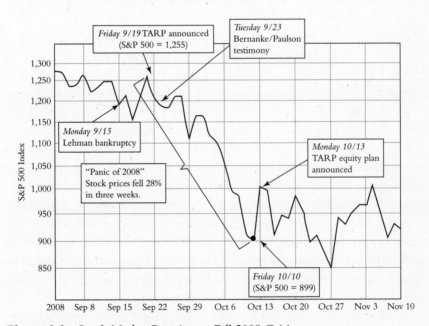

Figure 2.2   Stock Market Reaction to Fall 2008 Crisis
SOURCE: From TAYLOR/WEERAPANA. *Principles of Economics*, 6E. © 2010 South-Western, a part of Cengage Learning, Inc. Reproduced by permission. www.cengage.com/permissions.

Taylor finds a roughly analogous trajectory in the stock market (see Figure 2.2). After closing at 1,252 the Friday before Lehman's bankruptcy, the S&P 500 dropped below 1,200 on the Monday of the bankruptcy. But by Friday, the market had recovered to 1,255, slightly above its pre-Lehman bankruptcy level. The real drop came the following week, with the announcement of the TARP plan. The S&P 500 fell to a low of 899 on October 10 before temporarily rising with the announcement that the funds would be used to buy bank stock.

Although we need to be cautious about reading too much into this evidence, given the swirl of events occurring at this time, Taylor's analysis strongly suggests that the crisis cannot be attributed to the Lehman bankruptcy. Taylor himself concludes that the unpredictability of the government's response was the principal cause of the severe deepening of the crisis. An "ad hoc interventionalist government policy," as he put it in congressional testimony, "which was revealed for the world to see in the following weeks, was what caused the panic."[7]

Lehman's Road to Bankruptcy

As we have just seen, the conventional wisdom that the Lehman bankruptcy triggered the worst of the financial crisis falls apart if we consider the actual reaction of the market in September and October 2008. What about the other major component of the Lehman myth, the contention that bankruptcy failed, and that it is a disorderly and ineffective mechanism for dealing with the financial distress of a large financial institution? Here, too, the conventional wisdom is misguided.

The myth goes like this. Lehman's bankruptcy was a disaster, with much of Lehman's value—which the bankruptcy petition listed as $639 billion—vanishing when the petition was presented to the bankruptcy court. Its winding down was helter-skelter, as will always be the case if a large financial institution files for bankruptcy.

The most obvious problem with this reasoning is that it ignores the conditions under which Lehman filed for bankruptcy. The bailout of Bear Stearns six months earlier had sent a strong signal to the markets that the government would rescue any large nonbank financial institution that stumbled. During the summer of 2008, Lehman CEO Richard Fuld entertained offers from several potential purchasers, including Korea Development Bank (KDB). Fuld took a hard line in these negotiations, bargaining as if the buyers were the ones who were desperate for a deal. According to the definitive account of the crisis, Fuld blew up a deal that his lieutenants had carefully negotiated by insisting that KDB pay 1.5 times book value for Lehman's assets, rather than 1.25, and that it retain Lehman's real estate business rather than spinning it off.[8]

There no doubt were a variety of reasons for Fuld's complacency. Former colleagues describe him as relentlessly optimistic, even by the standards of investment bank CEOs. This optimism may have blinded him to the depth of Lehman's predicament, as its high leverage and exposure to the subprime real estate market brought Lehman to the precipice. "Dick was so proud of Lehman," as a friend put it, "that he was slow to recognize that others didn't share that belief." Fuld also had a large equity stake in Lehman. A substantial investment in Lehman by an outside buyer would significantly dilute his stake and the interests of other Lehman shareholders, including Fuld's fellow executives. If Lehman were purchased outright, Fuld would almost certainly be forced to give up control.[9]

While each of these factors surely played a part, another consideration backstopped everything else: Fuld was confident that the government would step in with rescue financing in the event all else failed. Lehman was several times larger than Bear Stearns, which had just been the beneficiary of government largesse; this made Fuld's confidence that the government wouldn't let Lehman go entirely logical. Fuld trusted that his personal relationships with Henry Paulson and other officials could be tapped in the event worse came to worst. In the summer of 2008, he told friends that he had a great deal of capital with Paulson, and he continued to believe that "Paulson was in his corner," as one early retrospective of the collapse put it, "even as the Treasury secretary publicly resisted spending taxpayer money to help Lehman."[10]

Given the expectation of a bailout, Fuld and Lehman had little reason to start making plans for an orderly bankruptcy, as they might be expected to do if they viewed bankruptcy as a plausible option. Indeed, an executive who thinks that his firm is a candidate for a bailout has every incentive to do precisely the opposite: to deliberately fail to plan for bankruptcy and to make bankruptcy as unattractive as possible, in order to persuade any government officials who might have second thoughts that a bailout is the only option.

Fuld wasn't alone in assuming that Lehman could count on a bailout. Lehman's potential buyers—which included Bank of America until it agreed to buy Merrill Lynch instead, as well as Barclays, the eventual purchaser—and just about everyone else fully expected a bailout as the bank desperately trolled for buyers in its final days. As Kimberly Summe has written, "many market participants continued to believe that either an acquirer would step forward or the government would assist the troubled firm as it had Bear Stearns."[11]

These expectations can be seen in the movement—or surprising lack of movement—in spreads for credit default protection against a default by Lehman on its bonds during the months immediately before it filed for bankruptcy.

As Figure 2.3 shows, the spread for credit default swaps on Lehman did not begin to rise until very shortly before Lehman filed for bankruptcy. The fact that prices for credit default swaps on Lehman stayed so stable in the summer and early fall of 2008, despite widespread perceptions that Lehman was financially precarious, strongly suggests that market participants expected the government to prop Lehman up if necessary, so that the credit default swaps would not be triggered. They expected Lehman to be another Bear Stearns.

This, then, is where things stood on the fateful weekend when Lehman's century-long tradition came to an end. By refusing to provide funding, Treasury Secretary Paulson and other regulators essentially dumped Lehman into bankruptcy, flouting everyone's expectations. Lehman could hardly have been less prepared. Indeed, a widely cited *Wall Street Journal* article calculated that Lehman squandered roughly $50 billion in value by eschewing any prebankruptcy planning; the financial advisers in Lehman's bankruptcy case put the number at $75 billion.[12]

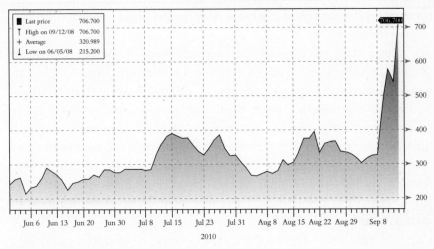

■ Last price	706.700
↑ High on 09/12/08	706.700
+ Average	320.989
↓ Low on 06/05/08	215.200

Figure 2.3 Lehman CDS Spreads
SOURCE: Bloomberg.

Lehman in Bankruptcy

Some of the immediate effects of the bankruptcy were jarring. Outside the United States, for instance, a number of Lehman subsidiaries were destabilized by the filing because they lost immediate access to their cash, which was cleared through a cash management system in New York. But credit for much of the damage belongs to the government, and its decision to pull the rug out from under Lehman after having signaled its intention to bail out troubled investment banks.

Moreover, despite having begun under the worst possible conditions, the bankruptcy process has been smoother and, where needed, faster than almost anyone could have anticipated. When a company files for Chapter 11, the managers continue to run the business, and most creditors are subject to the *automatic stay*—a rule that requires creditors to stop trying to collect what they are owed, in order to give the company a breathing space to begin dealing with the company's financial distress. (One major group that is not subject to the automatic stay is derivatives creditors—counterparties that have entered into derivatives contracts with the debtor.) Lehman and its lawyers—

Harvey Miller and Weil, Gotshal & Manges—have used this process quite effectively.

Three days after filing, Lehman arranged a sale of its North American investment banking business to Barclays, and the sale was quickly approved by the court after a lengthy hearing. Barclays provided a $450 million loan to fund Lehman's operations through the completion of the sale. As is common, the loan agreement required Lehman to appoint a professional turnaround manager to run the company. Its operations in Europe, the Middle East, and Asia were bought by Nomura, a large Japanese brokerage firm. By September 29, Lehman had agreed to sell its investment management business to two private equity firms.[13]

The Lehman bankruptcy illustrates several key features of current Chapter 11 practice. First, it shows that the law can facilitate an acquisition inside bankruptcy that would be troublesome outside bankruptcy. Barclays had expressed interest in Lehman prior to its filing, but would not acquire Lehman without substantial government assistance. After Lehman filed, Barclays was willing to purchase the assets it found most valuable, and also provided the financing required to keep Lehman liquid. The second feature is the speed with which acquisitions can be completed. Some commentators have argued that Chapter 11 is an inappropriate solution to distress because the process is too slow and costly. The Lehman case shows exactly the opposite: Faced with extreme time pressure, buyers materialized, and Lehman quickly sold its viable subsidiaries, allowing them to remain in business under different ownership.

Other commentators have expressed the opposite concern: that bankruptcy leads to an immediate dumping of assets. The fire sale of valuable assets at depressed prices in a bankruptcy reduces creditor recoveries, and can lead to failures in other firms that hold the same assets. This concern was an important motivation for the decision to extend rescue financing to AIG. Whatever its accuracy with AIG, the fire sale objection has no more support in the Lehman case than worries about bankruptcy delay. As of mid-2009, Lehman continued to hold a significant portfolio of assets, including a loan portfolio, real estate, and private equity investments. The firm's ability to obtain priority financing in bankruptcy allowed it to take time with these assets, and sell them into the market at times and prices that were driven more by value maximization than by a desperate scramble for liquidity.

Given the tumultuous environment in which Lehman filed its original bankruptcy petition, the assumption that bankruptcy must have been a disaster is perhaps understandable. But in fact, bankruptcy worked quite well. And it would work even better if the bankruptcy rules were adjusted in several respects, as we will see in Chapter 9.

Bear Stearns Counterfactual

Rather than Lehman's bankruptcy filing, the real pivot point in the crisis came when regulators decided to bail out Bear Stearns in March 2008. It was this decision that set the stage for the deluge that followed. One way to appreciate how the handling of Bear Stearns shaped the subsequent panic is to ask a simple question: How might the crisis have unfolded differently if regulators had not bailed out Bear Stearns?

As with Lehman, the Bear Stearns saga unfolded over a few crisis-packed days. After the markets lost confidence in Bear and its $18 billion of cash reserves began to disappear in early March 2008, Bear Stearns's chief executive, Alan Schwartz, called Timothy Geithner, who was then head of the New York Federal Reserve Bank. Geithner, then-Treasury Secretary Henry Paulson, and Ben Bernanke pushed Bear into the arms of JPMorgan Chase, a much healthier bank. The deal was structured so that the creditors of Bear Stearns were fully protected, Bear's shareholders took a serious haircut, and the government kicked in a $29 billion guarantee of Bear's most dubious assets.[14]

If regulators had decided not to bail Bear out, the default clearly would have stressed the markets. Regulators were particularly worried about the extremely short-term loans—known as repo loans—that investment banks depend on for financing. A repo loan is structured as a sale of securities by the borrower to the lender, with a promise by the borrower to buy the securities back later, often the next day. If there were a major default in this previously safe lending market, the market might have frozen up and major repo lenders that were not repaid might have been destabilized or even might have failed.

Some of these consequences might have come about if Bear hadn't been rescued, but the risk of widespread ripple effect collapses—also known as contagion effects or systemic risk—was almost certainly overstated. The creditors of Bear Stearns would have suffered losses, and the shareholders would have been wiped out. But this hard medicine would have sent a very clear message to the managers, creditors, and shareholders: Be careful whom you lend to, and watch what the company is doing, or you could get burned. In more technical terms, a Bear Stearns bankruptcy would have eliminated moral hazard—the tendency not to take precautions if you'll be spared the consequences of bad outcomes.

It also would have forced Richard Fuld of Lehman, as well as the executives of AIG, to think very differently about the implications of their firms' difficulties. The prospect of bankruptcy would have given them a very different perspective on how best to respond to financial distress. At the least, they would have gotten their books in order and started looking for buyers for their businesses much earlier and much more seriously.

By all accounts, Paulson, Geithner, and Bernanke never seriously considered stepping to the side and allowing Bear Stearns to file for bankruptcy. Why is this? One reason is that the mere whisper of systemic risk strikes fear into the hearts of financial regulators. If regulators agree to a misguided bailout, there are few immediate consequences. But if they forgo the bailout and the default infects other institutions, they could face a marketwide collapse and eternal condemnation. Given the stakes, regulators regularly overestimate the likelihood of systemic risk.

These particular regulators were even more wired for bailouts than most. As one would expect from a former head of Goldman Sachs, Paulson is a problem solver and deal maker. His instinct is to make a deal and move on. (Indeed, an interesting scholarly article analyzing the 2008 interventions referred to this as "government by deal.") Geithner cut his teeth in the international affairs division of the Treasury, and as a key underling to Larry Summers in the Clinton administration.

The 1990s saw two key crises that seem to have permanently shaped Geithner's instincts: Mexico's currency crisis in 1994 and 1995, and the collapse in 1998 of Long-Term Capital Management (LTCM), the giant hedge fund run in part by superstar economists. Both times, regulators opted for a bailout (funded by private banks in the LTCM case), and both were widely viewed as successful. Bernanke, as is well known, was a scholar of the Depression at Princeton prior to his appointment to the Federal Reserve. The mistake he vowed never to see repeated was being too tightfisted with government money in a time of crisis, as the Depression-era Fed was.[15]

A final factor was that none of the three had any experience with bankruptcy. Nor was there significant bankruptcy expertise in the Fed or Treasury. Ironically, one reason for this was the successful lobbying efforts in the 1980s and 1990s to insulate derivatives from the bankruptcy process—a special treatment I alluded to earlier in this chapter and will revisit in Chapter 9. This left little reason for bank regulators to learn anything about how bankruptcy works.

The prospect of bankruptcy at the end of the line would discourage excessive risk taking in the first instance, encourage creditors to monitor, and if dark clouds did develop, spur managers to make plans for an orderly bankruptcy. But none of this occurred during the summer of 2008, because regulators decided to bail Bear Stearns out.

Road to Chrysler

All of the events we have discussed thus far occurred on the Bush administration watch, of course. Even before President Obama took office, however, there was good reason to believe that his administration would continue and perhaps even extend the existing line of thinking. By bringing Geithner into his administration as secretary of the Treasury, Obama ensured that financial policy would be influenced by the most fervent advocate of bailouts during the Panic of 2008. Any doubt about the commitment to ad hoc intervention disappeared in the first few months of 2009, when the new administration made its own bailout decision with Chrysler and General Motors.

The Chrysler and GM bailouts were steeped in legally dubious maneuvering from the beginning. After the TARP legislation that authorized $700 billion in funds for the banking industry was enacted in October 2009, then-Treasury Secretary Paulson assured lawmakers that he didn't intend to use any TARP money to rescue the carmakers. "The TARP is aimed at the financial system," he told Congress on November 18; "in terms of autos, I have said it would not be a good thing." But he quickly changed course when it became clear that Congress had no stomach for an auto bailout. Paulson and the Bush administration pumped a total of $17 billion into the carmakers in late 2008 in order to fund their operations into the following year.[16]

By its terms, the TARP legislation permitted funding only of "financial institutions," which from a layperson's perspective the auto companies most assuredly are not. The question whether the definition was malleable enough to justify funding the auto industry was later raised by Indiana's pension funds when they challenged the Chrysler bankruptcy, but it was never decided. The bankruptcy court concluded that the pension fund was not a proper party to raise the issue, and the appeal was ultimately dismissed as moot by the Supreme Court.[17]

Shortly after he entered office, President Obama turned the negotiations with GM and Chrysler over to a new Auto Task Force, whose 14 members included Treasury Secretary Geithner, National Economic Council director Larry Summers, auto industry representative Ron Bloom, investment banker and Democratic party fund-raiser Steve Rattner, and 10 others. Bloom and Rattner directed much of the day-to-day work. (Although Rattner has been more loquacious about his role, the advisers I've spoken with suggest Bloom was the driving force.)[18]

By most accounts, there was a spirited debate on the Task Force whether to double down on the earlier rescue financing—particularly with Chrysler—or to cut off further funding. But to the surprise of few, the administration decided to bail out both companies, and thus to at least temporarily save an important industry in a politically essential state. Their strategy could not have been more audacious. They would try to persuade Chrysler's creditors to agree to a nonbankruptcy workout.

But if the creditors would not agree to the government's terms, the administration would use a so-called quick rinse bankruptcy to achieve the results they wanted. When senior Chrysler creditors balked at the sharp concessions they were expected to make, the government used the pretense of a bankruptcy sale to decide who would get what.

Chrysler Bankruptcy

The Obama administration's strategy for bailing Chrysler out was to file for Chapter 11, but to effect a sale of Chrysler's assets. In form, the sale was quite similar to the sale at the outset of the Lehman bankruptcy. But in reality, there would not be a real third party buyer. Fiat was sometimes described as the "buyer," but Fiat did not actually put up any money. The assets would be sold to a new shell corporation informally known as New Chrysler, and Fiat would receive a large block of its stock—initially 20 percent, potentially increasing to over 50 percent in the end—in return for agreeing to make its know-how and facilities available to New Chrysler.

The U.S. and Canadian governments would provide all the financing for the supposed sale, which would consist of a $2 billion payment to Old Chrysler, whose assets consisted of the scraps that were left over after the valuable assets went to New Chrysler, together with the $2 billion payment for the good assets. The $2 billion would go to Chrysler's senior lenders, who had a security interest in all of the original company's assets at the time of bankruptcy. This would pay them roughly 29 percent of the $6.9 billion they were owed.[17]

The terms of the deal struck with Fiat contain unmistakable evidence of the corporatist dimension of the rescue. As its initial stake, the government gave Fiat 20 percent of the stock of New Chrysler. But Fiat's stake will be bumped up to 35 percent if, among other things, Fiat causes Chrysler to roll out a new fuel-efficient (at least 40 miles per gallon) car in the United States. The government thus hardwired the Obama administration's energy policies into the terms of the rescue.

The transaction also seemed to pick and choose which creditors would be favored and which would not. Ordinarily, senior creditors must be paid in full before any other creditors are entitled to payment. Yet Chrysler's senior creditors were promised only 29 cents on the dollar, while several groups of lower-priority creditors would receive far less. Under the terms of the "sale" agreement, New Chrysler promised to give the union retirees a $4.6 billion note and 55 percent of the new company's stock in return for Chrysler's $10 billion in obligations to them. The agreement also assured creditors that $5.3 billion in ordinary trade debt would be paid in full. In contrast, Chrysler's future products-liability claimants—the victims of malfunctioning Chrysler cars—were not so fortunate. They would be cut off altogether.

Here was a radically new kind of bailout. With Bear Stearns, AIG, and other more traditional bailouts, the government paid most or all of the creditors in full. The government did not try to pick and choose among the company's creditors, favoring some and abandoning others. But with Chrysler, it rescued the company and at the same time made ad hoc decisions as to which creditors would be protected and to what extent. The sale seemed to flip well-settled priority rules on their heads and to completely abandon the ordinary rule-of-law principles that are the hallmark of the bankruptcy process.

As I have described the transaction thus far, and as it was condemned by its critics at the time, the Chrysler "sale" seems to have blatantly disregarded the requirements of American bankruptcy law. It did, but the abuse was more subtle than this description suggests. Unlike with the Bear Stearns collapse, which was overseen by regulators who knew little about bankruptcy and did not receive bankruptcy advice until it was too late, the Auto Task Force was advised by some of the nation's most prominent bankruptcy lawyers in the weeks before the decision was made to put Chrysler into bankruptcy. They structured the transaction in a way that was both brilliant and lawless.

In theory, the transaction might have been legitimate. If the Chrysler assets that were sold to New Chrysler really were worth only $2 billion, then $2 billion is all the senior lenders and other Chrysler creditors were entitled to. Yes, the reasoning would go, the unions and trade creditors did better than we might have expected, but this had nothing to do with their involvement in Old Chrysler. The payments to the unions and the trade creditors weren't being made by the original company; they were being made by the new company, which had bought the assets fair and square. The new company may look a lot like the old company (same plants, same cars, same unions), but it's a completely different company. If it wants to pay some of the creditors of the old company, that's the new company's business. Old Chrysler was worth $2 billion, in other words, and that money was properly distributed to the senior lenders. The unions and trade creditors didn't get any of this, so priorities were properly respected.

One problem with this reasoning is that the payments by New Chrysler to the unions and trade creditors were not simply based on an independent decision that New Chrysler made after it acquired all the good Chrysler assets. The payments were *required* by explicit contractual provisions in the sale agreement itself. The government insisted on it.[20]

But the more fundamental objection goes to the issue of whether $2 billion really was an adequate price to pay for Chrysler's assets. When a company proposes to sell most or all of its assets in bankruptcy rather than going through the traditional process of negotiating the terms of a reorganization plan, courts generally insist on a robust auction at which any interested bidder can make a bid. Courts also look to other protections to make sure that a sale fetches a fair price for the benefit of the company's creditors. With Chrysler, by contrast, the government made sure that a true auction could not take place.[21]

The Chrysler auction was about as far from a robust auction as one can imagine. To participate in the auction, bidders were required to submit a "qualified bid." What would count as a qualified bid? A bid that looked just like the government's bid, and gave the favored constituencies everything the government wanted them to get. If a bid didn't promise the same payout to the unionized employees' retirement fund—a $4.6 billion note, 55 percent of the buyer's stock—and if it didn't promise to pay $5.3 billion of trade debt in full, it wouldn't count as a qualified bid. This meant, for instance, that a bidder who wanted to offer $2.5 billion in cash for Chrysler's Jeep division would not be deemed to be submitting a qualified bid. The bid wouldn't be allowed.

When a creditor objected, the bankruptcy judge did prod Chrysler and the government into one small concession. If a bidder submitted a nonqualified bid, the debtor would consult with several other parties before deciding whether the bid would be considered. Which parties would the debtor consult with? Not just the creditors, but also the U.S. Treasury and the unionized employees. Notice the assumptions underlying this consultation: The government, labor, and the carmaker would jointly determine whether a bidder would be considered. Any bid that did not honor the partnership of the government, Chrysler, and labor obviously would be ruled out of bounds.[22]

Even apart from the failure to require a robust auction, there is a serious question whether the Chrysler transaction was a sale at all. Most of Chrysler's obligations were carried over to the new company and promised substantial or full payment. By any reasonable interpretation, this transaction was a corporate restructuring that needed to be conducted through the normal process of confirming a reorganization plan under Chapter 11—a process that provides far more protection for the company's creditors than a sale at the beginning of the case, which requires only the approval of the bankruptcy judge.

General Motors "Sale"

Although GM is a far more important company, its bankruptcy-bailout received far less attention. One reason is that GM and the government avoided several of the most controversial features of the Chrysler transaction. Unlike Chrysler, which stiffed the senior creditors, General Motors promised to pay its senior creditors in full. (It didn't hurt, in this regard, that GM's senior debt of $6 billion was smaller than Chrysler's.) GM also agreed to pay some of its tort claims, rather than cutting them all off as Chrysler had done to the consternation of many.

The GM transaction was hardly a paragon of rule-of-law principles, however. In several respects, it was even more dubious than Chrysler. Unlike Chrysler, which at least offered the pretence of a real sale to an actual buyer (although, as we have seen, the buyer, Fiat, didn't actually pay any money), GM didn't bring in any outside buyer at all. The so-called sale was purely a sale to self. To make sure that no troublesome bidders showed up at the auction, the court agreed to impose a qualified bid requirement. In GM's case, the requirement was even more stringent than in Chrysler's, since bids that didn't provide the same protections for favored constituencies as the government-crafted bid were ruled out altogether.[23]

It is hard to fault the bankruptcy judges in the Chrysler and General Motors cases. The government put them in an almost impossible position. Because the transactions were structured as sales rather than as ordinary Chapter 11 reorganizations, the bankruptcy judge was the only thing standing between the government and its objective both to bail out the auto industry and to decide which creditors would get paid and which would not. The government contended that Chrysler and GM were no different than other bankruptcy cases, except that the government rather than a private lender was providing the funding. But the cases were not ordinary at all. Indeed, they bore a striking resemblance to the sham sales that were a standard feature of corporate reorganization in the late nineteenth and early twentieth centuries. New Dealers like William O. Douglas (the Supreme Court justice and friend and poker partner of President Roosevelt) thought they had stamped out these practices, which they condemned as favoring insiders at the expense of ordinary investors, by reforming the bankruptcy laws in the 1930s. And yet another progressive administration reintroduced them 70 years later.[24]

From Myths to Legislative Reality

By telescoping the financial crisis into a single chapter, I obviously have offered a simplified account of the origins of the new financial legislation. An awful lot was happening in 2007 and 2008, and the events have been the subject of a number of very good, lengthy books and will no doubt spawn more.

Yet I have no doubt that the one factor that contributed more directly to the thinking of the architects of Dodd-Frank than any other was the Lehman myth. The key players repeatedly claimed, and seem to have believed, that Lehman's bankruptcy was the cause of all the woes that followed. All regulators needed, in this view, was more tools for intervening when a giant financial institution falls into financial distress. The carmaker bankruptcies added another dimension. By commandeering the bankruptcy process, the government was able to distinguish among otherwise similarly situated creditors, deciding which to pay and which not to pay.

As the debates on the legislation got under way in the spring and summer of 2009, the administration would fight for financial legislation that combined all of these features—the ability for regulators to intervene in ad hoc fashion, and the flexibility to decide whether to pay any given group of creditors. In the next chapter, we see how they managed to get nearly everything they wanted.

Part II

THE 2010 FINANCIAL REFORMS

Chapter 3

Geithner, Dodd, Frank, and the Legislative Grinder

A few decades ago, back when childhood games were as rough-and-tumble as Washington politics, we played a game in which one child ran through a gauntlet of his peers holding a soccer ball. He clung to the ball, and the rest of us tried to punch it out as he ran past. If he was still holding the ball when he emerged, he had won.

Watching the progress of the financial reform legislation from its origins in early 2009, I found myself thinking back to that childhood game. The Obama administration started with a basic framework—think of it as the ball—that was widely and correctly viewed as a bank-centered reform agenda that would establish a European-style partnership between the government and the largest banks. Treasury Secretary Timothy Geithner and his lieutenants—think of them as the boy—clung to the agenda as they were pummeled in hearings and in the press. By the end of the year, a few commentators were clamoring for Geithner to be replaced as Treasury secretary. But President Obama never wavered in his support either for Geithner and Larry Summers, the other mastermind behind the legislation, or for the basic regulatory approach. Although the administration was forced to make adjustments at key junctures, the basic framework survived essentially intact. They won, leaving their stamp on financial regulation for the next generation.

In this chapter, we revisit the twists and turns that led to the Dodd-Frank Wall Street Reform and Consumer Protection Act of 2010. I recount some of the key moments in the debates—such as President Obama's endorsement of the Volcker Rule as the legislation's architects gritted their teeth, and the Securities and Exchange Commission's decision to sue Goldman Sachs, which removed any lingering questions whether the legislation would pass. The goal of the chapter is not so much to provide a moment-by-moment retrospective as to highlight the principles underlying the administration's framework and to show how the framework was shaped by the legislative process. This will provide the necessary context for an in-depth analysis of the key components of the legislation in the chapters that follow.

The Players

The two architects of the legislation from within the administration were Treasury Secretary Tim Geithner and Lawrence Summers. Geithner's emergence as the public face of the administration's financial reforms, and thus as the lead actor, is a coming-of-age of sorts. During the Clinton administration, Summers was the Secretary of the Treasury and Geithner was a key underling of Summers (and before that, of Robert Rubin, Summers's predecessor as Treasury Secretary), serving in the international affairs division. But if one of the two is the senior partner in the current administration, it is Geithner.

After Geithner's career at Treasury, he decamped to the Council on Foreign Relations and then a high-level position at the International

Monetary Fund. In 2003, he was named president of the Federal Reserve Bank of New York, the post that thrust him into the center of the financial crisis in 2008. Two key events during Geithner's tenure at Treasury seem to have made an indelible impression on him: the Mexican currency crisis of 1994 and 1995, when Mexico nearly defaulted on its debt; and the collapse of Long-Term Capital Management (LTCM), a giant, star-studded hedge fund, in 1998. In each case, regulators opted for a bailout (funded by private banks in LTCM's case), and both bailouts are widely viewed as successful interventions. Mexico's crisis passed, and LTCM's collapse had little evident lasting effect on the market, although both contributed to later crises. The lesson Geithner seems to have learned is that bailouts are the best response when a large institution or country is in trouble. By all accounts, he pushed hard for the Bear Stearns bailout and he spearheaded the disastrous American International Group (AIG) rescue. In a scathing front page story highlighting Geithner's cozy relationships with the largest banks and his reputation as a "bailout king," the *New York Times* reported with incredulity that he had even "proposed asking Congress to give the president broad power to guarantee all the debt in the banking system" during the summer of 2008.[1]

Given Geithner's contributions to the Bush administration's response to the financial crisis, and especially his fingerprints on the $182 billion AIG bailout, he seemed an unlikely choice to be tapped for high-level service in the Obama administration. But his extensive experience at Treasury in the last Democratic administration, as well as President Obama's desire for continuity in responding to the financial crisis, both weighed in his favor. Most importantly, the two bonded immediately, no doubt in part due to their mutual comfort with governance by elites and comparably cool demeanors in a crisis.

Summers arrived at the White House after several years in the woodshed. A year after remarking at a scholarly conference that scientists should study the possibility that men are genetically more inclined to scientific intelligence than women, he was forced to resign as president of Harvard University. Many thought his career as a public figure was over. But he rehabilitated himself by writing regular columns in the *Financial Times* during the economic crisis—the liberal economist and pundit Paul Krugman called them "must reads." He soon found himself advising the Obama campaign, and though Summers probably would not have been confirmable as secretary of the Treasury, President Obama brought him in as director of the National Economic Council, a position that didn't require Senate approval.

Together, Geithner and Summers were the economic point men for the administration, the advisers who constructed the administration's framework for regulatory reform. Geithner especially is comfortable and experienced at backroom negotiations with the chief executives of the banks that dominate the financial markets. As already noted, both hail from the corporatist side of American economic thinking. Although President Obama has deliberately assembled groups of competing advisers in other areas—a strategy inspired by Presidents Roosevelt and Lincoln—there was no high-level advocate of downsizing the largest financial institutions to encourage more competition. Even the de facto head of the new Consumer Financial Protection Bureau, Elizabeth Warren, is said to have told an aide during the legislative debates that "the only people Obama listens to" on economic issues are Geithner and Summers.

In Congress, the key figures on financial reform were the chairmen of the House Financial Services and Senate Banking committees, Representative Barney Frank and Senator Christopher Dodd. In early 2010, facing a tough reelection campaign, Dodd announced his retirement from the Senate at the end of the year. Some speculated that this would heighten his sensitivities to the interests of the Wall Street banks, since retirement might find him working on or lobbying for Wall Street, while others predicted that freedom from the need to solicit Wall Street contributions would toughen his stance. But the biggest effect seems to have been to magnify the legislation's personal significance to Dodd as a legacy. Frank might have been more inclined to press for an alternative stance—he had, for instance, been a major critic of the partial repeal of the Glass-Steagall Act—but he, too, was anxious for a major financial overhaul to pass. Although Frank pressed for constraints on the largest financial institutions at times, both he and Dodd followed the administration's lead.

TARP and the Housing Crisis

On February 10, 2009, a month before he rolled out the first version of the financial reform legislation, Geithner took the podium for a much-publicized speech on a separate but overlapping part of the administration's response to the financial crisis. In retrospect, the speech and the initiatives it announced foreshadowed both the administration's vision for financial reform—and what would be left out.

The speech itself was a disaster. The *New York Times* reported that "lobbying associations for the banking and financial services companies praised Mr. Geithner's plan as bold and far-sighted." Investors, in contrast, "were far more restrained. The stock market dipped almost as soon as Mr. Geithner began speaking, with the Dow Jones industrial average down about 350 points, or more than 4 percent, at 1:30 P.M." The principal complaint was vagueness: "analysts and private investors said they simply did not know enough to make a judgment on the plan's prospects."[2]

Despite the unflattering reviews, one of the initiatives—the stress test—proved remarkably successful. Later in the spring, when the results were announced, the stress tests identified 10 of the 19 biggest banks as needing to shore up their capital by a total of $75 billion overall, but concluded that the banks were all basically sound. To the surprise of many, given the widespread suspicion that the stress tests were a sham (the Geithner character in a *Saturday Night Live* skit announced, for instance, that he had decided to forgo the old-fashioned pass-fail grading system, and just make it "pass-pass"), the stress tests reassured the markets and reassured market participants that the banking system was out of the woods, at least temporarily. The use of Troubled Asset Relief Program (TARP) funds to replenish bank capital in late 2008 and the 2009 stress tests are now regarded as the steps that stabilized the banks.[3]

The administration's housing initiative—known as the Home Affordable Modification Program (HAMP)—by contrast, has proved far less effective. Framed as an overhaul of the Bush administration's even less effective program for helping homeowners modify their mortgages, HAMP promises fees to mortgage servicers that agree to modify homeowners' mortgages. Eligibility is subject to a number of restrictions, however, and banks have continued to resist major modifications. As of summer 2010, only 340,000 mortgages had been permanently modified under the $50 billion program.

Both the banking stress tests and the earlier capital infusion were primarily backward-looking, dealing with the fallout of the crisis, whereas the Dodd-Frank legislation establishes a new regulatory framework for the future. But both the capital infusions and the stress tests have important implications for understanding the new legislation. The first is the distinction between industry-wide and ad hoc strategies for dealing with struggling financial institutions. The capital infusions and stress tests were an industry-wide response to the crisis. In contrast, the resolution rules that lie at the heart of the new legislation, like the bailouts of Bear Stearns and AIG, are an ad hoc, firm-specific response to financial distress. As we will see in Chapter 8, the optimal strategies in the two contexts are quite different. Most importantly, the need for industry-wide support in a financial crisis does not justify bailouts of individual firms. As the debates on the financial reforms began, Geithner seemed to treat the two as interchangeable.

The lesson of the housing program involves bankruptcy as a response to the financial crisis. From the outset of the housing crisis, it was clear that the most effective strategy for providing relief for homeowners would be to amend one small part of one bankruptcy rule. Under current law, a homeowner who files for bankruptcy cannot reduce the amount of his or her mortgage to the current value of the property. Unlike almost any other loan, mortgages cannot be altered in bankruptcy. Changing this rule and treating mortgages like other loans would have made it far easier for homeowners to restructure their mortgages. Although banks fended off this reform during the Bush administration, the Obama administration was widely expected to insist on the reform. But it didn't. The failure to push this reform underscores both the surprising pull that the largest banks have in the Obama administration and the puzzling aversion to bankruptcy-based reform.[4]

Road to an East Room Signing

The template that would eventually become the Dodd-Frank legislation was released by Treasury in March 2009, immediately before a major convocation of the G-20 nations in London. Entitled "Rules for the Regulatory Road," the proposal identified four major areas of focus: addressing systemic risk, protecting consumers and investors, eliminating gaps in the regulatory structure, and fostering international coordination. Nearly all of the concrete proposals focused on the first issue, addressing systemic risk. The proposal called for a singling out of systemically important firms like Citigroup or AIG for several kinds of a special oversight. According to the proposal, these institutions should be overseen by a single, independent overseer, although Treasury withheld judgment whether the Federal Reserve or some other regulator would get the job; they should be subject to heightened capital requirements; and Congress should enact a special resolution framework giving regulators the power to step in and take over floundering systemically important institutions. The proposal also called for comprehensive new regulation of the over-the-counter (OTC) derivatives markets and for registration of hedge funds.[5]

The most fully developed component of the initial proposal was the new resolution rules. The proposed rules would give the Treasury Department the power to intervene when systemically important banks and nonbank financial institutions fall into financial distress and to appoint the Federal Deposit Insurance Corporation (FDIC) to restructure or liquidate them. They also authorized bank regulators to provide funding for a troubled firm either before or after the FDIC stepped in. The overall effect would be to extend the sweeping, largely uncontestable authority the FDIC has over troubled banks to bank holding companies and other financial institutions.

Both the resolution rules and the overall framework read as if they had been written by Timothy Geithner in consultation with the large banks he had worked with as head of the New York Fed. Geithner would get all of the powers that he and former Treasury Secretary Henry Paulson wished they had had when they intervened with Bear Stearns, Lehman Brothers, and AIG. But the framework also did not overly ruffle the feathers of the largest financial institutions. There was no call to break them up, as commentators like MIT professor Simon Johnson and Nobel laureate economist Joseph Stiglitz had been advocating. While systemically important status might subject the biggest institutions to greater oversight, it also would bring benefits in the marketplace. They could borrow money more cheaply than could smaller competitors, because lenders would assume they would be protected in the event of a collapse, as the creditors of Bear Stearns and AIG were.

The suspicion that the legislation might be a little too accommodating to the largest banks was further aroused by the discovery that Davis, Polk & Wardwell, "a law firm that represents many banks and the financial industry's lobbying group," as the *New York Times* put it in the article that broke the story, and which Geithner had hired to handle the AIG bailout on behalf of the New York Fed, had been deeply involved in the early drafting of the legislation. Treasury had worked from a draft first written by Davis Polk, and the legislation literally had the law firm's name on it when Treasury submitted it to Congress, thanks to a computer watermark that Treasury had neglected to delete.[6]

In June 2009, three months after the Treasury proposal, the Obama administration released the fully developed package, which included all the major components of what eventually became the Dodd-Frank Act. As outlined in a detailed Treasury White Paper, the administration proposed that the Federal Reserve be given primary regulatory responsibility for systemically important financial institutions, and that Congress establish an oversight council consisting of the heads of the principal financial regulators to monitor systemic risk. For systemically important firms—described as "Tier 1 financial holding companies," Treasury further developed the other features that had been included in the earlier proposal: higher capital requirements and a special new resolution regime.

The White Paper's biggest surprise was a new proposal for a consumer financial protection agency. The agency had been conceived by Harvard law professor and TARP Oversight Committee head Elizabeth Warren, first in a short 2007 article whose title—"Unsafe at Any Rate"—consciously linked her to the Ralph Nader crusades of the 1960s, and then in a more detailed, co-authored article a year later. Warren acknowledged that existing regulators already had ample authority to protect the interests of consumers, but she argued that the existing structure all but assured tepid oversight. Most importantly, the Federal Reserve, the principal regulator, has a deep conflict of interest when it comes to consumer protection: The Fed's principal concern is the safety and soundness of the banking system; banking profitability and health may be furthered by the very practices (such as high credit card fees and deceptive mortgage practices) that consumers need to be protected against.[7]

How did the new agency, which wasn't even hinted at in the earlier template, suddenly show up as a key pillar of the administration's proposed legislation? Not because Timothy Geithner had developed a passion for consumer protection. Indeed, he and Warren clashed on several occasions at hearings before the TARP Oversight Committee in the ensuing months. The magical moment seems to have been a long lunch Warren had with Larry Summers at an Indian restaurant in Washington, D.C., in April 2009. Summers didn't make any promises, but Warren came away from the meeting convinced that he was on board. And indeed he was.[8]

Adding the consumer protection agency had cross-cutting effects on the debate. On the plus side, it heartened the administration's liberal supporters, many of whom believed that the proposed reforms went too easy on Wall Street. On the negative side, it complicated the administration's efforts to persuade Republicans and moderate Democrats to support the legislation. The wild card was the question whether the agency would eventually be dropped, as many thought it would. (Travis Plunkett, the legislative director at the Consumer Federation of America and a leading advocate of the agency, was so nervous that he kept watch in the Senate building, lingering in the hallways until 4 A.M. on the morning Senate Democrats hashed out the final terms of the bill in June 2010, for fear the agency would be gutted or removed.)[9]

Although many of the key reforms were relatively uncontroversial—including far-reaching changes such as a requirement that derivatives be cleared and traded on exchanges—proponents of the legislation faced two repeated challenges in the months that followed. The first, and most incessant, was the allegation that the resolution regime would institutionalize and extend the bailouts of 2008. It would simply give regulators more tools for bailing out the next tottering giant financial institution. And by explicitly labeling some firms as systemically important, it could actually increase the number of firms treated as too big to fail. Second were complaints that the legislation did nothing to get the largest Wall Street banks under control, either by breaking them up or by limiting their ability to gamble on derivatives and other risky investments.

The obvious alternative to the administration's resolution framework would be tailoring bankruptcy to handle large nonbank financial institution distress. In the hearing held before the House Judiciary Committee, Harvey Miller, the lead lawyer in the Lehman and General Motors cases, forcefully advocated this approach. Although Miller was scheduled to testify separately, the Judiciary Committee invited him to join the two administration regulators who testified first in order to defend the benefits of a bankruptcy-based alternative. Miller argued that the proposed resolution rules were cumbersome and unnecessary, and that bankruptcy was a much preferable solution—particularly if the laws were amended to remove the special treatment of derivatives (a topic we take up in Chapter 9). "No rationale is given" was how he put it in the written version of his testimony, "for why the existing bankruptcy law and bankruptcy courts could not deal with the resolution of . . . financial crises." Miller was lavishly praised by Representative John Conyers Jr. and other members of the Committee, and his written testimony was widely circulated in the months that followed.[10]

The repeated attacks on the resolution framework as institutionalizing bailouts forced the administration to adjust the framework to make it look more like bankruptcy. In the versions that were passed in the House of Representatives in December 2009 (the Frank Bill) and in the Senate the following March (the Dodd Bill), the resolution rules gave regulators the power to retrieve preferential payments made to creditors on the eve of default, as in bankruptcy, and incorporated a handful of other bankruptcy rules as well.[11]

Even after these bankruptcy-mimicking features were added, the resolution regime still was and is an agency-oriented approach far removed from bankruptcy. The FDIC will have sweeping authority, with only limited transparency and minimal judicial review of its decisions. Given the hostility to bailouts, why didn't lawmakers shift their attention to bankruptcy? Why wasn't Chapter 11 ever a contender?

Two possible answers will immediately occur to anyone who has read the earlier chapters of this book: The Lehman myth seemed to call the efficacy of bankruptcy into question, and the Treasury Department had a strong preference for regulatory rescues and an equally strong aversion to bankruptcy. The two factors often traveled together, of course. Secretary Geithner and his associates repeatedly invoked the Lehman myth as they made their case for expanding regulatory powers. In the hearing discussed earlier, Assistant Treasury Secretary Michael Barr leaned heavily on Lehman, insisting that "as Lehman's collapse has showed quite starkly, and as I will discuss in some detail today, there are times when the existing options under the Bankruptcy Code are simply not adequate."[12]

While these factors can explain the *administration's* resistance to bankruptcy, however, they don't tell us why *Congress* didn't take up bankruptcy in earnest. In nearly every context in which I heard it raised, among both Democrats and Republicans, there was genuine interest in a bankruptcy alternative. The Democratic leadership obviously wouldn't have bucked the White House lightly, but even this wasn't the most important reason that bankruptcy didn't get off the ground, despite a widespread willingness among lawmakers to consider it. The real reason was much deeper and more mundane: committee jurisdiction.

It was simply inconceivable that either Representative Frank or Senator Dodd or their committees would relinquish their reins over the reform process. If the reforms contained a significant bankruptcy component, they would be forced to do just that—that is, lose their grasp over the reforms. Bankruptcy legislation is the prerogative of the Judiciary Committees, while financial reform belongs to the Senate Banking and House Financial Services Committees. As a senior aide whose boss was a major figure in the debates put it in an e-mail to me and two others: "We feel strongly that bankruptcy can and would work for most financial institutions but have stumbled onto the difficult challenge of the . . . jurisdictional issues between Judiciary and Banking."[13]

With bankruptcy off the table but complaints about the bailouts continuing to roil the debate, the administration and Senator Dodd took additional measures to make the resolution rules look less like a framework for bailouts. Unlike in the earlier Treasury White Paper, regulators would not be permitted to reorganize the financial institutions they took over under the resolution rules; the only option would be liquidation. The administration and Senator Dodd also added provisions imposing the cost of any resolution on the banking and financial services industry—not taxpayers. And when Republicans contended that a $50 billion assessment that would be set aside for resolution was essentially a bailout fund, the fund was removed. By the end, the debate whether the framework would foster bailouts, as Republicans claimed, or would prevent them, the Democrats' mantra, reached comic dimensions. Senator Barbara Boxer, a Democrat from California, proposed an amendment saying regulators would never, ever do anything but liquidate a troubled financial institution under the resolution framework. The amendment was criticized as redundant, and passed overwhelmingly.

Channeling Brandeis: The Volcker Rule

In addition to bailouts and debates over how much authority the Federal Reserve should get, the other major brush fires centered on concerns that the legislation did little to rein in the dominant Wall Street banks. Remarkably, particularly for a Democratic administration that modeled itself on Roosevelt's New Deal, no one in the administration's inner circles had advocated handcuffing or breaking up the largest banks.

In the Roosevelt administration's Brains Trust of leading advisers, advocates of corporatist-style partnership between the government and large institutions had jostled for supremacy with advisers who wanted to break up the large institutions in order to ensure vibrant competition in every industry. Rex Tugwell and Adolph Berle, both Columbia professors, were the most vocal corporatists, while Louis Brandeis, the Boston lawyer and then Supreme Court justice, pressed for measures that would break up the so-called Money Trust—the large banks that dominated American finance—and encourage competition. While both sides won victories at times, the signature New Deal financial reforms were Brandeisian: the Glass-Steagall Act broke up large Wall Street banks like J.P. Morgan by severing commercial banking (deposits and loans) from investment banking; and deposit insurance made smaller banks more competitive, since deposits would be just as safe in small banks as in large ones.

Unlike Roosevelt, President Obama simply did not have any Brandeisians in the house: he, Geithner, and Summers all have corporatist leanings. The problem for the administration is that many Americans were suspicious of the corporatist dimension of the legislation. The financial institution bailouts of 2008 remained deeply unpopular, and there was a widespread perception that the government had nursed Wall Street through the crisis but hadn't done much to help the folks on Main Street. By the end of 2009, the Obama administration was considering ways to address these concerns in the legislation. But it took a single climactic event to force the President's hand: the election on January 19, 2010, of Republican Scott Brown to fill Ted Kennedy's Senate seat in Massachusetts. The Brown election, which threatened to derail the health care legislation, was interpreted as evidence of a populist wave in American politics.

In a speech on January 21, President Obama endorsed a proposal by former Federal Reserve Chair Paul Volcker that would prohibit deposit-taking banks from engaging in proprietary trading—that is, trading for their own accounts. Congress should enact this "simple and common-sense reform," he said, "which we're calling the Volcker Rule—after this tall guy behind me." The imposing, six-foot-eight Volcker had been a key economic adviser during the presidential campaign, an éminence grise who lent gravitas to Obama's economic platform. But he had faded from the inner circle after the election, and had little or no role in the framing of the financial legislation—becoming so invisible as the legislation made its way through Congress that he was the subject of a "whatever happened to Volcker" story in the *New York Times*. With the Brown election, however, the administration threw its support behind the Volcker initiative.[14]

Another populist moment came several months later, when Arkansas Senator Blanche Lincoln, who was facing a tough primary challenge from her left in the Democratic party, shepherded an amendment through her agricultural committee that would forbid commercial banks from dealing in derivatives. In its strongest form, this would have prevented any holding company that included a commercial bank subsidiary from trading in derivatives anywhere in the holding company network. In weaker form, it would have forced the holding company to put the derivatives in a separate subsidiary. The Lincoln amendment also made its way into the Dodd Bill.

The Goldman Moment

As late as April 2010, the fate of the Dodd Bill and the legislation generally was still uncertain. On April 19, the Securities and Exchange Commission (SEC) sued Goldman Sachs, alleging that Goldman had duped investors in a complex transaction called Abacus by failing to tell them that hedge fund manager John Paulson had helped to choose (and was betting against) the mortgage-related securities at the heart of the transaction. The decision to sue was controversial at the SEC, with the three Democratic commissioners voting yes and the two Republicans no. But the outrage at Goldman, which had already become an emblem of Wall Street hubris, gave the legislation irresistible momentum. Within a few weeks the Dodd Bill would pass the Senate, and a conference committee was set up to reconcile it and the Frank Bill from the House.

Neither the Volcker Rule nor the Lincoln amendment fully survived into the final bill. The Volcker Rule was watered down by an amendment needed to secure the vote of Scott Brown—the very senator whose election had inspired its inclusion. Under the amended Volcker Rule, banks will be permitted to invest up to 3 percent in hedge funds or private equity funds. And the Lincoln amendment was changed to a complicated set of rules (described in plain English in Chapter 5) that allows banks to trade derivatives as long as the derivatives operations are cordoned off in a separate entity from any ordinary banking operations. An amendment by Senator Susan Collins added limitations on banks' debt—and thus, their riskiness—in some circumstances.

The restrictions on banks take a half-step away from the corporatism favored by Geithner and Summers, apparently in a Brandesian direction. But the nature of the half-step makes all the difference. Each of the restrictions depends heavily on how it is ultimately implemented by regulators. (Regulators have two years to implement the Volcker Rule, as many as three for the Lincoln amendment.) This discretion will give regulators additional clout in their partnership with the biggest financial institutions, but there is little reason to believe the giant banks will downsize in any significant way. Ironically, the restrictions could actually *reinforce* the partnership between regulators and the big banks by creating an ongoing negotiation over the banks' operations. Perhaps even more surprising, the new Consumer Financial Protection Bureau, which the banks fear most of all, could end up having a somewhat similar effect.

In the chapters that follow, we take a much closer look at the key components of the Dodd-Frank Act, and explore each of the implications just described.

Chapter 4

Derivatives Reform: Clearinghouses and the Plain-Vanilla Derivative

E veryone from the *Huffington Post* to Henry Paulson agrees that derivatives and the other new financial innovations of the past several decades exacerbated the financial crisis. As Bear Stearns's financial stability deteriorated in March 2008, largely due to its heavy stake in mortgage products, regulators fretted that a Bear Stearns default would throw the repo market into turmoil. Things didn't get much better in the months that followed. Concerns about the consequences of American International Group's inability to make good on an explosive portfolio of credit default swaps (CDSs) in which it had insured interests in mortgage-related securities were a major justification for the $182 billion bailout. The mortgage-related securities held by Bear

Stearns and insured by American International Group (AIG) were themselves the product of recent financial innovation.[1]

I should pause here to note that I have lumped together at least three different elements of contemporary finance in my reference to "financial innovations." The Dodd-Frank Act homes in on the first of these innovations, derivatives, which were both touted as a savior by former Federal Reserve Chairman Alan Greenspan and denounced as "weapons of financial mass destruction" by Warren Buffett prior to the recent crisis. A derivative, as we have seen, is simply a contract between two parties whose value is based on changes in an interest rate, a currency, or almost anything else, or the occurrence of a specified event. The second innovation is the structured finance, or securitization, transactions that produced the mortgage-backed securities we now think of as toxic assets. In a mortgage securitization, mortgages are sold to a new entity (the special purpose vehicle), which purchases the mortgages with funds obtained by selling securities in the new entity to investors. The securities held by investors—as well as by banks like Bear Stearns—are the mortgage-backed securities. Finally, investment banks like Bear Stearns and Lehman Brothers used very short-term repo transactions—sales of securities with a promise to repurchase them later at a higher price—to finance their operations.

None of these innovations, either individually or collectively, was the real cause of the financial crisis. The crisis stemmed from the overheating of the real estate markets, due among other things to artificially low interest rates and policies designed to promote home ownership, which included political pressure on Fannie Mae and Freddie Mac to expand the range of consumers who would have access to mortgages. The Dodd-Frank Act simply sidesteps the question of what to do with the now government-owned Fannie Mae and Freddie Mac. Almost the only reference to the problem in the 2,319 pages of the Act is a provision commissioning a study.[2]

While derivatives, securitization, and repos didn't cause the crisis, each exacerbated it due to perversities in the way these markets functioned. The Dodd-Frank Act almost completely ignores the repo market—whose short-term financing transactions were used by Lehman to manipulate its books, and created the contemporary equivalent of bank runs—an omission we discuss in Chapter 5. Dodd-Frank did add a few new regulations dealing with the most obvious problem with mortgage securitization, as we will see in Chapter 6.

But Dodd-Frank devoted far more attention to the first of the innovations, derivatives. In this chapter, we consider the entirely new regulatory structure that Congress has now erected for derivatives.

Basic Framework

Here, in summary form, are some of the key features we will be considering:

- Instruments covered: swaps and security-based swaps.
  - The Commodity Futures Trading Commission (CFTC) regulates swaps.
  - The Securities and Exchange Commission (SEC) regulates security-based swaps.
- Institutions subject to special oversight: swap dealers and major swap participants.
- Key innovation: clearinghouses and exchanges:
  - Clearinghouse:
    - CFTC and SEC decide if a swap must be cleared.
    - Clearinghouse backstops both parties.
    - Clearinghouse sets margin requirements.
- Exchanges (and swap execution facilities):
  - Swaps must be presented to exchange if clearing is required.

Prior to the Dodd-Frank Act, the regulatory framework assumed—in part through historical accident and in part through design—that the derivatives markets were essentially self-regulating. For privately negotiated, over-the-counter (OTC) derivative contracts, there was little disclosure or regulatory oversight. A special set of bankruptcy exemptions assured that, if one of the parties filed for bankruptcy, the other party would not be prevented from seizing collateral or terminating the contract. This freedom from regulation, and the increasing role of derivatives and other financial innovations as mechanisms for borrowing money, gave rise to their characterization as a shadow banking system.

Due largely to historical accident, jurisdiction over derivatives is divided between the CFTC and the SEC. The Dodd-Frank Act preserves this distinction, dividing derivatives between swaps, which are regulated by the CFTC, and security-based swaps, which are the purview of the SEC. Except to describe this division, I will refer to both as swaps for simplicity throughout the chapter.

The most important derivatives innovation of the new legislation is a new clearing requirement that gives the CFTC and SEC the power to require that any category of swaps be cleared. When a derivative is cleared, a third party—the clearinghouse—agrees to stand behind both parties, guaranteeing each party's performance to the other.

Swaps that are cleared must also be presented to an exchange (defined in Dodd-Frank as a "board of trade") for exchange trading. To be traded on an exchange, a derivative must be standardized so that it functions like a share of stock on the New York Stock Exchange, rather than a contract negotiated by two parties in private. Both the clearing and the exchange requirements will dramatically alter prior practice, in which most derivatives were private contracts negotiated between two parties, and were subject to very little regulation.

The first big question mark of the new regime is whether most derivatives will indeed migrate to clearinghouses or exchanges, or whether the major banks will persuade regulators that they are too complex and specialized for clearing and exchange trading. The second is how the clearinghouses will function. If the new framework has untoward side effects, they almost certainly will involve a crisis with one or more of the clearinghouses.

Because the eccentricities of the prior framework are the product of accident and history, I will begin with a brief historical overview. I then consider how the derivative markets and their regulation will (and won't) be transformed by the new legislation, looking first at the clearinghouses and exchanges and then at their regulators.

Derivatives and the New Finance

The derivatives and other financial innovations that became so important to the banks' bottom lines at the end of the twentieth century were regulated under a framework whose roots go back many decades. (As is often the case in finance, one can trace the antecedents of today's derivatives back thousands of years; the origins of the modern regulatory framework are, however, of rather more recent vintage.) U.S. regulation was shaped by pitched battles in the late nineteenth and early twentieth centuries between the emerging markets for futures contracts in corn and other commodities and populist critics who believed that these markets were simply a new form of gambling. Of particular concern in the early debates were bucket shops—small, local operations set up for speculating in commodities contracts. According to critics, the participants in these markets were "devils in their gambling hells." Populists complained both that commodities trading was gambling and that the operators of bucket shops were scoundrels who fleeced their unsuspecting customers. The organized exchanges, such as the Chicago Board of Trade and the Chicago Mercantile Exchange, agreed with the populist condemnation of bucket shops while insisting that commodities trading on an organized exchange was perfectly legitimate.[3]

Until the 1920s, the principal regulatory intervention came from judicial interpretation of permissible and impermissible futures contracts. Drawing on an old line of English cases, some courts held that a futures contract was unenforceable if the parties did not intend the commodity in question actually to be delivered at the end of the contract. If the parties agreed to simply net out the difference between the value of the commodities at the beginning and end of the contract period—which the English cases referred to as a contract for differences—they were really just speculating. Only if the buyer genuinely intended to acquire the commodity was the contract legitimate. In 1905, the Supreme Court seriously weakened this line of attack on derivatives contracts in a case called *U.S. Board of Trade of Chicago v. Christie & Stock Co.* The *U.S. Board of Trade* case held that futures contracts were enforceable so long as the contract had a serious business purpose; it wasn't necessary that there be an actual intent to deliver.[4]

Congress finally stepped in during 1922 and then again during the Depression. With the Grain Futures Act of 1922, Congress sought to stamp out the bucket shops (and gave the exchanges much of what they wanted) by making futures contracts illegal unless they were traded on exchanges. In 1936, Congress enacted the Commodity Exchange Act, which created a federal regulator—the Commodity Exchange Commission, which in 1974 would be restructured into the current Commodity Futures Trading Commission. One of President Roosevelt's principal objectives in promoting the 1936 regulation was to fill in a regulatory gap left by securities acts enacted in 1933 and 1934. The securities acts, which created the Securities and Exchange Commission and gave the SEC the power to police speculation on the securities markets, didn't cover the Chicago grain exchanges. As speculation diminished on the securities exchanges, it seemed to shift to the grain exchanges. The enactment of the Commodity Exchange Act ensured that there would be a regulator to police commodities contracts, just as there was with securities. The addition of a second regulator made perfect sense at the time, but led to destructive regulatory turf battles later in the century.

As of the late 1930s, one could fairly confidently say that futures contracts—the principal derivatives of this era—were perfectly legal if they were traded on one of the exchanges but generally illegal if they were not. Yet by the end of the twentieth century and beginning of the twenty-first, almost all of the derivatives action was off the exchanges. A huge amount of the derivatives trading volume was in over-the-counter (OTC)—that is, non-exchange-traded—derivatives.

The reversal was sealed by a now-famous retrenchment in derivatives regulation at the behest of the leading investment banks, their trade groups, and major derivatives participants like Enron. As swaps and other new forms of derivatives proliferated in the 1980s, the CFTC initially took a laissez-faire stance, issuing "no action" letters assuring the derivatives industry that the CFTC would not challenge the trading of these contracts outside of the exchange, and creating an explicit safe harbor for qualified swaps. To the extent there was a principled basis for stepping aside and letting the derivatives industry take care of itself, the reasoning seems to have been that the parties to these contracts were the largest and most sophisticated of Wall Street banks. They were capable of taking care of themselves.

But in 1998, CFTC head Brooksley Born unsettled the now-established understanding by questioning the hands-off tradition and threatening to subject the market to closer supervision. Born was already viewed as somewhat suspect by the other key financial and securities regulators, both because she did not have the same Wall Street credentials and because the CFTC and SEC were engaged in an increasingly contentious turf battle as to which regulator would have jurisdiction over the new derivatives, many of which could be characterized as either commodities (the CFTC's domain) or securities (the SEC's). To the other regulators—U.S. Treasury Secretary Robert Rubin, Federal Reserve Chair Alan Greenspan, and SEC Chair Arthur Levitt—Born's threat of intervention was an outrage, a gratuitous slap at a crucially important market that could be destabilized by the intrusion. To quell Born's revolt, Rubin, Greenspan, and Levitt took the extraordinary step of issuing a joint press release warning that additional regulation could be catastrophic.[5] Coming at a time when Rubin was President Clinton's most important financial adviser and almost godlike powers were attributed to Greenspan, Born didn't have a chance. She quickly backed down, and OTC derivatives remained unregulated.

Although Born had been chastened, nothing formally prevented her or the CFTC from regulating the rapidly expanding OTC derivatives market. The derivatives industry remained at risk. In 2000, at the end of the Clinton administration, the industry persuaded Congress to explicitly protect the most important categories of OTC derivatives from regulation. Under the Commodity Futures Modernization Act, a broad range of derivatives—including swaps and mortgage-related derivatives—were explicitly excluded from both CFTC and SEC regulation.

In retrospect, we can see that the protection that the leading derivatives dealers, led by Goldman Sachs, secured in the 2000 legislation had two major consequences. First, it protected a huge source of profits for the banks. Because OTC derivatives are not standardized and are negotiated on a contract-by-contract basis, the dealer banks can charge very large fees for arranging them. According to one recent accounting, U.S. banks generated $1.9 billion in the second quarter of 2009 and $1.2 billion in the third quarter from credit derivatives (a category that does not include interest or currency swaps) alone. This income, more than risks to the market or any other factor, is what really was at stake in the fight over regulation. And this is why the banks are so worried about the effort in the new legislation to push more derivatives onto exchanges.[6]

The second effect was to exacerbate the financial crisis. The opacity of the derivatives markets and fears that the markets would freeze up paralyzed regulators at each crisis point during the Panic of 2008. Regulators had no idea how much exposure Bear Stearns and Lehman had as they tumbled toward default. They also worried that a Bear Stearns default would create chaos in the credit default swap market, because there were so many CDS contracts purporting to insure the protection buyers against a default by Bear on its bonds. Fears about the effect of canceling the large portfolio of credit default swaps in which AIG promised to insure against defaults on mortgage-backed securities was one of the principal rationales for the huge AIG bailout. Regulators almost certainly overstated the systemic risks of a Bear Stearns or AIG default. But the opacity of the market and its potential fragility, particularly given that it was dominated by a small number of banks, were all too real.

The Stout Alternative

The new clearinghouse and exchange requirements occupied an unusual status in the recent legislative debates: They were sweeping and yet remarkably uncontroversial. I exaggerate a little. They did attract some critical comment—particularly at the outer reaches of their scope— and the major Wall Street banks lobbied quietly and actively to soften the requirements. But the basic principle that derivatives should be traded on exchanges if possible, and nearly all should be cleared, had widespread support. The general consensus extended both to the scholarly literature and to lawmakers.

Scholars being scholars, clearinghouses were not the only proposed solution to the problem of an opaque and unregulated derivatives market. Among legal scholars, University of California at Los Angeles law professor Lynn Stout proposed nearly a decade before the crisis that lawmakers sweep away the tortured history of derivatives regulation and return to the original common-law rule that "contracts for difference"—contracts in which one party agrees to pay the other based on the change in value of a commodity, currency, or anything else—are simply unenforceable. Denying enforcement might seem to be a recipe for destroying the derivatives market, since nearly every derivative would come under the prohibition. But Stout argued that the markets would continue to operate, even in the face of nonenforcement, for the same reasons that gamblers wager in states in which gambling is legal but gambling contracts are unenforceable: As long as the other party can be trusted to make good on the contract, it is of little moment that the contract would not be enforceable in court.[7]

As Stout envisioned its effect, not only would her scheme simplify regulatory oversight, but the risk of nonenforcement also would dampen purely speculative derivatives trading, and it would encourage the parties to deal with counterparties that had a strong reputational stake in making good on their contracts. One obvious concern with the proposal is that it could exacerbate (or at the least preserve) the concentration of the derivatives industry. Firms that wished to enter into derivatives contracts would have a strong incentive to deal with repeat players—since these parties would have the greatest reputational interest in making good on their contracts. The leading repeat players are, of course, the five banks that dominate derivatives trading. The proposal might also discourage the exchange trading of derivatives. Because the value of any given derivative would depend on the creditworthiness of the counterparty, otherwise identical derivatives could have different values.

The proposal can be viewed in another way as well—in a fashion that brings it into closer alignment with the strategy adopted by the Dodd-Frank Act. In addition to dealing with repeat players, firms that deal in derivatives would surely set up collateral arrangements to protect against the risk that their counterparty might default. The collateral arrangements might look similar to the margin requirements that clearinghouses are expected to establish under the Dodd-Frank Act.

New Clearinghouses and Exchanges

I have emphasized that the new clearinghouse and exchange regimes reflect a near consensus among scholars and commentators. The vision is hardly self-executing, however. Under pressure from groups such as industrial firms that use derivatives, lawmakers made a series of decisions regarding whom to exempt and whom to include, and left others to regulators. We begin with the framework that emerged, which regulates nearly all swaps, and then turn to the risks that the clearinghouses themselves may pose.

The first major distinction wired into the Act is a concession to the existing regulatory division between the CFTC and SEC. The Act provides separate but parallel treatment of swaps and security-based swaps; swaps correspond to the derivatives that currently come within CFTC jurisdiction, and security-based swaps correspond to those the SEC regulates. (Currency swaps, interest rate swaps, and credit default swaps all qualify as swaps; only swaps dealing with stock and other securities—a contract based on the difference between the current and future market price of a stock or index of stocks, for instance—constitute securities-based swaps and come within the SEC's domain.)[8]

For the big Wall Street banks that dominate the market, Dodd-Frank creates two new regulatory labels: swap dealers and major swap participants. A swap dealer is any entity that holds itself out as a dealer in swaps, makes a market in swaps (that is, arranges for the other parties to enter into swaps), or regularly enters into swaps. At the least, this will cover the major dealer banks—Bank of America, Barclays Capital, Citigroup, JPMorgan Chase, and 11 others. A major swap participant is any firm that "maintains a substantial position" in the swaps markets. ("Substantial position" does not include hedging transactions, which will let companies that buy derivatives simply to protect against price changes, as airlines do with oil derivatives, escape the "major swap participant" designation.) The principal cost of qualifying as a swap dealer or major swap participant is new capital and margin requirements.[9]

The basic requirements of the new regime are straightforward. If regulators conclude that a swap should be cleared, it must be presented to a clearinghouse for clearing and to an exchange (or "swap execution faculty") for trading. Although it received much less attention in the media coverage of the Dodd-Frank Act, the migration of swaps to exchanges may be more costly for the largest banks—assuming that swaps do indeed migrate—than clearing. Prior to the new legislation, most swaps were privately negotiated, based on standard forms created by the International Swaps and Derivatives Association, and were steered away from exchanges by design. Because the derivatives were individually tailored, the banks could charge big fees—far more than with a plain-vanilla, exchange-traded derivative. If most swaps do make their way to exchanges, the largest Wall Street banks stand to lose a large portion of these profits.

Regulatory Dilemmas of Clearinghouses

The clearinghouse requirement is closely analogous, but raises issues that go still more directly to the risk-reducing objective of the new legislation. If Goldman Sachs and Bank of America enter into an interest rate swap that is required to be cleared, for instance, they must select a clearinghouse to serve as a middleman in the contract. The clearinghouse then assumes responsibility for the performance of both parties. This means that Goldman has much less reason to worry about Bank of America's stability when it enters into the swap, and vice versa; most of the risk now belongs to the clearinghouse. To protect itself against nasty surprises, the clearinghouse will require both parties to post margin—payments or collateral that the clearinghouse can sell if the counterparty defaults on its obligations. (Margin payments consist of "initial margin," which is set aside at the outset, and "variation margin," which is adjusted daily to reflect changes in the expected value of the contract.)[10]

The clearinghouse arrangement is premised on the assumption that most or all derivatives will be cleared. This will be up to the CFTC and SEC, who decide whether a particular type of swap must be cleared (and thus both cleared and exchange traded). Most likely, the regulators will err on the side of requiring clearing, but it is not hard to imagine Wall Street banks trying to persuade regulators two or three years from now that clearing and exchange trading are not suitable or necessary for some new derivative. Banks will benefit if they can limit the migration to clearinghouses and exchanges, and they are in a position to make the migration less rather than more likely by creating derivatives that are difficult to standardize.[11]

As of the end of 2009, two years into the crisis, the major dealer banks reported that 35 percent—$202 trillion—of the total notional amount of OTC interest rate derivatives were cleared, and that another 43 percent could plausibly be cleared. (The notional amount is the value that serves as a baseline for the contract, rather than the amount either party owes.) They announced a commitment to clear 70 percent of new interest rate derivatives trades. Given that interest rate swaps are often among the most generic of derivatives, these figures suggest that a substantial percentage of derivatives could go uncleared. If the slippage were substantial, we would be more or less back where we were before Dodd-Frank, with the possibility of substantial counterparty risk if the bank or one of its counterparties with a large, uncleared exposure threatened to fail.[12]

But I suspect that a large majority of derivatives will find their way to clearinghouses and exchanges within a few years. Indeed, the transition was already under way—in part spurred by the prospect of new regulation, to be sure—even before Dodd-Frank was enacted. (A leading derivatives scholar who shares the view that the migration will indeed occur recently predicted to me that 60 percent would be cleared within a year, 80 percent within four years.)[13]

Suppose the new clearing requirement does indeed cause the migration of most derivatives to clearinghouses. This does not mean that the risk of the derivatives markets will simply evaporate. The magnitude and shape the risk takes will depend on how the market for clearinghouses develops. If one or two clearinghouses dominate the market, each will be a source of major systemic risk. If more clearinghouses enter the market, clearinghouses could face some of the same perverse incentives that marred credit rating agency oversight before the crisis. This second possibility—a multiplicity of clearinghouses— is the more worrisome of the two.

Start with the possibility of a dominant clearinghouse. As of this writing the securities exchanges all have clearinghouses, and there are several others as well. Suppose one of these—or another that is not yet a glimmer on the financial landscape—secures a dominant share of derivatives clearing. With the clearinghouse in place, the parties to a derivatives contract will have much less need to worry about one another's finances, since the clearinghouse is responsible for both parties' performance. But this means that the clearinghouse itself will become an enormous source of systemic risk.

The emergence of a few dominant clearinghouses is in fact the most likely scenario, because a party with significant derivatives business will be required to provide less collateral if all of the derivatives are cleared in one place. Being a party to several derivatives spread out over several clearinghouses requires posting margin to each clearinghouse. Putting up collateral to only one clearinghouse—and then only for the net exposure from all of the dealer's transactions with that clearinghouse—will be more profitable. Although this effect would be mitigated if clearinghouses were to cooperate with each other on behalf of a major counterparty for each, the Dodd-Frank Act explicitly allows a "just say no" reaction to such a proposal by a clearinghouse. If they cannot cooperate easily with each other, both competition and economies of scale will naturally lead to a few very concentrated clearinghouses.[14]

How likely is it that one of these clearinghouses might fail? The Dodd-Frank Act tries to minimize the danger by requiring every clearinghouse to maintain a minimum financial reserve large enough to cover the default of its largest participant and to continue operating for at least a year after the default. In contrast to the vague guidelines for collateral requirements, the potential loss from default by the largest participant is a fairly concrete number, which a clearinghouse could calculate on a daily basis. But the financial reserve is keyed to only one large participant. There is no reason to believe the reserve would be adequate if more than one large participant failed at the same time, as of course was precisely what happened during the Panic of 2008. Moreover, the CFTC (and SEC, for security-based swaps) has been given primary responsibility for overseeing the clearinghouses, although the Fed is authorized to participate in some functions. Unlike the Federal Reserve, which has the sophistication to regulate the clearinghouses' risk, the CFTC has appreciably less expertise.[15]

The consequences of a giant clearinghouse failure are almost unfathomable. As we saw earlier, banks' derivatives business totals $291 trillion in notional value. A clearinghouse failure, which would of course be triggered by the instability of one or more banks or other large financial institutions, would be like the simultaneous failure of multiple systemically important banks. It could make the failures of 2008 look quaint by comparison.

No doubt in view of this, the drafters of Dodd-Frank have given the Federal Reserve the authority to lend to the clearinghouses, and thus the capacity to bail them out. The largest clearinghouses will thus be added to the roster of entities that are too big to fail.[16]

Despite the enormous concentration of risk, the emergence of one dominant clearinghouse might be more desirable than a multiplicity of clearinghouses. Although this clearinghouse would be a source of major systemic risk, regulators might be better able to detect problems with the clearinghouse. Banks are enormously complicated, conducting a wide range of activities, which makes them very difficult to oversee. Clearinghouse operations are not simple, but the clearinghouse focuses on a single type of business. It is not nearly as opaque as a bank. It is at least plausible that regulators would effectively police a dominant clearinghouse's risk—though the dominance comes at the cost of adding another massive entity that is too big to fail.

The alternative possibility—a multiplicity of competing clearinghouses—could lead to a dangerous race to the bottom in oversight. Prior to the financial crisis, the contention that more vigorous competition can have pernicious consequences would have required substantial explanation. But the breakdown of credit rating oversight now serves as an all-too-vivid illustration of what can go wrong. The entrance of Fitch Ratings into a market previously dominated by Moody's Investors Service and Standard & Poor's (S&P) severely undermined whatever discipline the credit rating agencies brought to the market for mortgage-related securities by inviting a practice that became known as ratings shopping. If an investment bank wanted to sell mortgage-related securities, for instance, and was unhappy with the ratings that Moody's or S&P signaled that it would give to the securities, the bank could simply take its business to Fitch. The ability to shop among multiple rating agencies created a race to the bottom, in which the agencies had to give generous treatment lest they face a serious loss of business.[17]

A similar dynamic could emerge with clearinghouses. If there are multiple clearinghouses, the clearinghouses may compete for business by lowering their standards. This could mean accepting substandard derivatives for clearing, setting inadequately low margin or collateral requirements, or both. These tendencies would increase both the risk and the consequences of a clearinghouse collapse. Ironically, the CFTC and SEC could exacerbate these dangers if they insist that nearly every derivative, even the most idiosyncratic, be cleared.

Even absent a race to the bottom, a proliferation of clearinghouses would remove an important tool for managing risk: the netting of offsetting obligations. If numerous derivatives involving the same parties are cleared on the same clearinghouse, the clearinghouse can match the various parties' gains on some contracts against their losses on others in the event of a default, reducing the overall exposure of the clearinghouse. But if the contracts are cleared on a large number of different clearinghouses, the ability of any single exchange to take advantage of the risk reduction benefits of netting will be greatly reduced.

Dodd-Frank doesn't ignore the risks of the clearinghouse process altogether. It requires, for instance, that the clearinghouse set adequate margin standards. But this requirement is more hortatory than specific. The legislation also invites regulators to address potential conflicts of interest by curbing the voting rights or ownership interests of systemically important financial institutions that have a stake in a clearinghouse.

These requirements may be helpful as well. But the effectiveness of the oversight regime will depend a great deal on the vigilance of the CFTC, SEC, and Federal Reserve.[18]

Disclosure and Data Collection

Before we conclude, we should consider one more dimension of the new framework: its requirements for disclosure and data collection. Disclosure and information flow problems have plagued the derivatives markets, and in fact contributed to the Fed's and Treasury's panic when Bear Stearns threatened to default in 2008. The new legislation ratchets up disclosure in three different ways. First, it creates a new entity known as a swap data repository to handle the large anticipated volume of new disclosure. The clearinghouses themselves are required to set up swap data repositories as part of their clearing operations. Second, swap dealers and major swap participants are required to register with the CFTC (or SEC, for trading securities-based swaps). Finally, the Act requires that the volume and prices of every swap be reported, in real time with non-cleared swaps and "as soon as technically possible" with cleared swaps.[19]

The new data and reporting requirements unquestionably will give regulators better access to information about derivatives trading and the major participants. The SEC's near complete ignorance of the operations of Bear Stearns and Lehman Brothers was one of the great regulatory embarrassments of the crisis.

The principal question is how much of the information will be disclosed publicly, and how quickly. Even before Dodd-Frank, when data was often limited, credit default swaps were often the best predictor of a company's financial condition. (One exception was credit default swaps on major derivatives dealers like Lehman Brothers, which were distorted by expectations of a bailout, as we have seen.) Dodd-Frank will generate far more information, and the data repositories are instructed to publish the information without identifying details. If meaningful information is indeed released—yet another "if" that will be up to regulators—it could provide an important supplement to regulatory oversight. Given the vagueness of the public disclosure requirements, however, there is a very real risk that the market for non-exchange traded derivatives will remain nearly as opaque as it was before the crisis.

Making It Work?

It all comes down to the regulators. That's one way of looking at the new derivatives regime. Everyone agrees that derivatives regulation could hardly have been worse than it was at the time of the crisis, and that the shift to clearing and exchange trading is an improvement. But the verdict is still out on just how large a portion of the derivatives market does indeed make the migration. It is possible that a substantial portion will remain outside the core of the new system. How this plays out will depend on the vigilance of the CFTC and SEC.

If most derivatives trading does wind up with clearinghouses, as it probably will, another set of issues emerges. On one hand, if there are numerous clearinghouses, the Wall Street banks may direct their business to clearinghouses that cut corners—or indeed, many of the clearinghouses may cut corners, as the rating agencies did—unless the CFTC and SEC police technical details like margin requirements more proficiently than they've done in the past. On the other hand, if there is a single dominant clearinghouse, the too-big-to-fail issue will take center stage. If a handful of large clearinghouses emerges, regulators may be faced with both sets of issues.

Even if the SEC and CFTC (with the Fed ever in the background with funding as needed) manage to do all these things well, there's also the prospect that derivatives traders evade the new framework by shifting overseas. We will consider several extraordinary and rather desperate provisions that were included in Dodd-Frank with this problem in mind later, in Chapter 10.

The success of the new derivatives regime is thus surrounded by question marks. On one hand, the Dodd-Frank Act's treatment of these instruments is one of the more promising contributions of the Act. Its treatment of the institutions that dominate the markets for derivatives, on the other hand—the giant banks like Citigroup and Bank of America, and their nonbank peers—is far more troubling. It is to this trouble that we now turn.

Chapter 5

Banking Reform: Breaking Up Was Too Hard to Do

A recurrent refrain throughout the debates that led to the Dodd-Frank Act was: "What will it do about Citigroup?" Citigroup was widely viewed as so sprawling as to be ungovernable, and as dangerously unstable. Among many of the congressional staffers I talked to, the acid test for any proposal was what it would mean for the future of Citigroup.

Historically, there have been two different strategies for managing the risk of the largest financial institutions, as we saw in Chapter 3. The first relies on a partnership between government and the dominant firms in an industry. The second—Brandeisian or Jeffersonian—tradition seeks to break up dominant firms to promote competition.

Dodd–Frank stands squarely in the first, more corporatist tradition. The administration and its congressional allies decided to single out the largest firms for special attention, and to subject them to higher capital requirements. The vision of government pacification of and partnership with the largest financial institutions that lost during the New Deal has resurfaced 75 years later and emerged triumphant. Although the administration was forced to make several concessions to its Brandeisian critics, even these concessions are more likely to cement the partnership between the government and the largest banks than to curb the banks' dominance.

Basic Framework

Here, in summary form, are some of the key features we will be considering:

- Principal regulators: Federal Reserve, Financial Stability Oversight Council.
- Institutions subject to special oversight:
  - Bank holding companies with $50 billion or more in assets.
  - Systemically important nonbanks (designated by Treasury and two-thirds vote of Financial Stability Oversight Council).
- Effect of inclusion:
  - Higher capital requirements.
  - Federal Reserve to determine requirements.
- Volcker Rule:
  - Prohibits banks from proprietary trading.
  - Limits stake in hedge funds or equity funds to 3 percent.

The principal regulatory oversight for the too-big-to-fail institutions will come from the new Financial Stability Oversight Council and the Federal Reserve. Any commercial bank holding company with $50 billion or more in assets will automatically be included in the group of systemically important banks that are subject to special oversight. With nonbanks, the decision is made by the Council, which will include the heads of all of the major financial regulators. If two-thirds of the voting members of the Council, including the secretary of the Treasury, vote to designate a nonbank like American International Group (AIG) as systemically important, it will be added to the club and subjected to the "more stringent" oversight planned for the largest institutions.

The most immediate effect of designation is to bring the institution under the umbrella of Federal Reserve oversight. The principal regulatory tool at the Fed's disposal will be to impose higher capital requirements on these institutions, in view of the risk the failure of one of these institutions might pose to the financial system.

The most widely discussed of the handful of provisions I will call Brandeisian concessions—that is, provisions that are intended to limit the size or expansion of the systemically important firms—is the Volcker Rule. The Volcker Rule prohibits bank holding companies from engaging in propriety trading (trading for their own accounts) and limits their ownership stake in any hedge fund or equity fund to 3 percent. In theory, this will limit banks to commercial banking activities.

I will take up the features of the new regulation in roughly the order just described, starting with the designation of systemically important financial institutions and the new regulation they will be subject to, and then turning to the Brandeisian concessions. The theme that will recur throughout the discussion is corporatism. The partnership between the government and the largest financial institutions—a partnership in which the government can and will channel political policy through the systemically important firms—will be the defining feature of the new financial order.

New Designator and Designatees

One of the most dramatic regulatory innovations of Dodd-Frank is the creation of a new Financial Stability Oversight Council. Chaired by the secretary of the Treasury, the Council will include the heads of each of the major financial regulators—including the Federal Reserve, the Securities and Exchange Commission (SEC), and the new Consumer

Financial Protection Bureau—as well as an independent representative of the insurance industry. The Council's general objective is to identify systemic risk and to ensure that appropriate oversight is in place to limit the risk of a systemic failure.[1]

The establishment of a new systemic risk regulator had been on the wish list of most reformers from the outset of the financial crisis. It was a central feature, for instance, of the Blueprint for a Modernized Financial Regulatory Structure released by Henry Paulson's Treasury Department in the last year of the Bush administration, and of every proposal that followed. The principal questions were what powers a systemic risk regulator should have and how its powers should be integrated with those of other regulators.

The Dodd-Frank Act divides authority over systemic risk and systemically important institutions between the Financial Stability Oversight Council and the Federal Reserve. The new framework for regulating systemically important institutions consists of two basic steps. The first is a determination of which firms should be subject to special oversight. The second issue is how to manage the risks posed by these firms.

For bank holding companies, the first step is automatic. Any bank holding company that has at least $50 billion in assets automatically qualifies as a member of the club. For nonbank financial institutions like AIG, the Council makes the determination whether to include them. To designate a nonbank financial institution, two-thirds of the Council members (including the secretary of the Treasury) must vote in favor of the designation, based on a conclusion that "material financial distress at the U.S. nonbank financial company, or the nature, scope, size, scale, concentration, interconnectedness, or mix of the activities . . . could pose a threat to the financial stability of the United States." Although the institution can challenge its designation, challenges are highly unlikely to succeed. Only if the designation is "arbitrary and capricious" will it be overturned by a court.[2]

The drafters of Dodd-Frank were well aware of the concern that a process for designating systemically important firms could lead to distortions in the financial services markets. Banking expert Peter Wallison of the American Enterprise Institute repeatedly warned in the

Wall Street Journal, in congressional testimony, and elsewhere that the approach would create a stable of new Fannie Maes and Freddie Macs, each of which would be able to borrow money more cheaply than other firms because of the perception they wouldn't be allowed to fail. "The result will be devastating for competition," he wrote in one of his commentaries. "Larger firms will squeeze out smaller ones and aggressive small companies will have less opportunity to overcome the government-backed winners."[3]

The claim that the largest financial institutions can borrow more cheaply than their smaller peers is confirmed by substantial evidence. As of 2009, large banks paid 0.78 percent less for funds than their peers, compared to 0.29 percent in 2000–2007.[4] (Lawmakers' vulnerability to too-big-to-fail criticisms may explain the bland terminology they adopted in Dodd-Frank. Rather than referring to the targeted firms as "systemically important" or even as Tier 1 holding companies, as in the original Treasury White Paper, Dodd-Frank simply identifies them as "a bank holding company with total consolidated assets of $50,000,000 or more, or a nonbank financial holding company supervised by the [Fed] Board of Governors.")

The principal concession to the Wallison concerns—and the strategy for limiting the likelihood that one of the firms will default—is a requirement that the designated firms be subject to higher capital standards than other comparable firms. Capital requirements are the buffer a bank or other financial institution is required to maintain to ensure its solvency. Or as Secretary Geithner recently put it: "Capital requirements are the financial equivalent of having speed limits on our highways, antilock brakes and airbags in our cars, and building codes in communities prone to earthquakes."[5] The value of a bank's stock counts as capital, for instance, whereas debt generally does not.

"In order to prevent or mitigate risks to the financial stability of the United States that could arise" from the distress of systemically important financial institutions or their "ongoing activities," the legislation instructs the Federal Reserve to impose "more stringent" capital requirements on these firms. While the Act provides only limited marching orders for what the enhanced standards must look like—a limitation we consider in more detail later—it does signal that strict capital requirements will be the strategy of choice for regulating the largest institutions. The rationale for higher capital standards is two-fold. It functions as a restriction on systemically important firms, an impediment that offsets to some extent the leg up they enjoy due to the perception they are too big to fail. The higher standards also limit these firms' ability to take risks with their assets.[6]

Will the New Capital Standards Work?

In its emphasis on higher capital requirements, Dodd-Frank is well within mainstream academic opinion on how best to rein in systemi-cally important firms and limit the danger of another meltdown. At every academic conference I have attended during the financial crisis, capital requirements have been the reform of choice. The 15 promi-nent economists who wrote *The Squam Lake Report*, for instance, which was released a few days before the Dodd-Frank Act was enacted, concluded that large banks should have higher capital require-ments because "potential systemic problems are bigger if the same risky positions are aggregated in one large bank rather than spread among several small banks." (*The Squam Lake Report* also proposes that capital requirements be stiffened for banks that hold hard-to-sell assets or whose financing is short-term and can be quickly taken away; in each case, the bank may be forced to sell assets at fire sale prices, which can depress prices to the detriment of any institution that holds similar assets.)[7]

Dodd-Frank's enhanced capital requirements have two serious lim-itations. First, it is devilishly difficult to calibrate capital requirements effectively, given the complexity of banks' balance sheets. The prec-risis capital requirements established under Basel II, which produced an international framework followed by European banks and with some qualifications by American banks as well, are a case in point. Although the Basel II capital rules were thought to be state-of-the-art, they did not require a bank to hold as much capital if it borrowed money through risky, off-balance-sheet financing arrangements as when it borrowed the same funds directly, thus encouraging the use of derivatives-based finance. The Basel II experience is an object lesson illustrating that the general enthusiasm for higher capital requirements is misplaced if the requirements cannot be implemented effectively.

Second, Dodd-Frank provides only limited instructions to the Federal Reserve for fulfilling its charge to impose higher capital requirements on systemically important institutions. The most explicit instructions come as part of a provision known as the Collins amendment, because it was offered by Senator Susan Collins. The Collins amendment is designed to impose on all systemically important institutions capital rules similar to those that apply to ordinary banks—and which call for tightened capital requirements as the bank's risk or leverage increases. But Dodd-Frank explicitly invites the Fed to exempt nonbank financial institutions from these restrictions. And other than a series of instructions to ratchet up a company's capital requirements based on the nature of its assets and liabilities, the extent of its off-balance-sheet exposure, and other factors, the Fed is left to its own best judgment in implementing the capital requirements.[8]

The new legislation thus delegates its signature initiative for reining in the banks to the Federal Reserve, which means that the capital requirements will be negotiated with the giant banks over the next few years. Perhaps the Fed will impose stringent capital requirements that fully offset the advantages of financial institutions that are perceived as too big to fail. But this seems unlikely. The institutions can credibly argue that stiff capital requirements will undermine their ability to compete with foreign financial institutions, thus hurting American finance. They will also argue that higher capital requirements will dampen the systemically important banks' willingness to lend. (Interestingly, although this argument makes intuitive sense, several recent studies suggest that higher capital requirements have very little effect on the volume of lending.)[9] The details will be technical and the negotiations will take place outside of the glare of Washington scrutiny, after public attention shifts from the financial reforms to other concerns. The likelihood that they will emerge with favored status surely is a major reason that the largest banks did not squawk much as Dodd-Frank's capital requirements and resolution regime were put in place.

In addition to the impact of the new capital requirements, the other central issue for the regulation of systemically important financial institutions is the Volcker Rule and several other Brandeisian provisions in the new law. The implications of these provisions will take up much of the rest of our discussion. But first, we shift our attention to something completely different.

Contingent Capital Alternative

Tucked into the details of Dodd-Frank's treatment of systemically important firms, along with the multitude of studies and reports called for by the Act, is a promising strategy for making automatic, midstream adjustments to shore up the balance sheet of a floundering financial institution. The strategy, which has generated considerable interest at the New York Fed during the crisis, is known as *contingent capital*. Although it is not formally adopted, the new legislation not only instructs the General Accountability Office to conduct a study; it invites the Fed to begin making use of contingent capital as soon as the study is complete.[10]

If a bank were subject to contingent capital, it would issue debt that would automatically convert to stock if the bank's capital fell below a specified level. (Under another triggering strategy, the conversion would occur if the bank defaulted on its debt.) The contingent debt would thus automatically replenish the bank's capital if its fortunes deteriorated, forestalling the need to sell assets or for an insolvency procedure. The strategy could be adapted for any kind of corporation—indeed, earlier versions were proposed not just by banking scholars, but by bankruptcy experts as well—but it is particularly attractive for financial institutions, given the systemic consequences of their failures.

Presented in summary fashion, as I have just done, contingent capital may sound like a perfect solution to the risk that a systemically important financial institution will fail and wreak havoc on the financial system. The mechanics are of course not quite as effortless as I have portrayed them. A contingent capital requirement that is triggered by a decline in the bank's capital will not be especially effective if the bank can easily manipulate its capital, or if capital requirements are low. Contingent capital also will not protect against a sudden collapse, as in the cases of Bear Stearns and AIG—a collapse that occurs so quickly and so pervasively that the new capital would come too late to break the fall.[11]

As the limitations suggest, contingent capital is not a complete solution to the risks posed by systemically important institutions. But it is a promising supplement to the Dodd-Frank framework. Lawmakers should be given credit for providing a nudge forward to a more revolutionary strategy than Congress ordinarily adopts, particularly given that it reintroduces a market role into a framework that relies so heavily on regulators.

Volcker Rule

The general framework that I have outlined thus far—nearly all of which can be traced to the administration's early proposals—has a distinctly corporatist flavor. It automatically identifies bank holding companies with $50 billion in assets as systemically important, and invites the Financial Stability Oversight Council to add large nonbank financial institutions. This new club of too-big-to-fails is put into partnership with the Fed and the systemic risk Council.

Several of the features that were added to the legislation in response to populist pressure hail from a very different place—the Brandeisian perspective that the administration rejected. To put these provisions into context, it will be useful to describe the arguments of the most forceful advocates of Brandeisian perspectives.

Throughout the financial crisis, MIT professor and former International Monetary Fund (IMF) economist Simon Johnson insisted that the largest banks—starting with Citigroup—should be broken up. Johnson points out that dominance of the largest banks is recent, dating only to the mid-1990s, with some of it stemming from distressed acquisitions during the recent crisis. Bank of America has grown from $1.7 trillion to $2.3 trillion in assets, in part through its acquisition of Merrill Lynch; JPMorgan Chase, buyer of Bears Stearns and Washington Mutual, has increased by $400 billion to $2.0 trillion.[12]

Johnson proposes to chop the financial giants down to size by imposing a "hard cap" on how large a bank can be. Under Johnson's approach, as outlined in his and James Kwak's book *13 Bankers*, commercial banks would be prohibited from growing to larger than 4 percent of the U.S. gross domestic product (GDP), and investment banks would be limited to 2 percent of GDP—which translates to $570 billion and $285 billion, respectively, in assets as of 2009. For riskier banks—he cites Goldman Sachs, given its heavy reliance on proprietary trading—Johnson would set a lower size limit. Aggressively enforcing these limits, he argues, would halt the increasingly oligopolistic structure of the financial services industry. It would "finish the job that [Theodore] Roosevelt began a century ago" when he broke up the great Standard Oil trust, and "take a stand against concentrated financial power just as he took a stand against concentrated industrial power."[13]

Other Brandeisians take their inspiration from Franklin rather than Theodore Roosevelt, and the New Deal's successful breakup of J.P. Morgan and it peers in the Money Trust of the early twentieth century through the Glass-Steagall Act's prohibition on combining commercial and investment banking in the same bank. Calls for a return to Glass-Steagall, which was largely repealed in 1999, began early in the crisis, but they were not taken especially seriously until Mervyn King, the head of the Bank of England, endorsed a very similar approach. King argued that the "utility-like" dimensions of banking, such as taking deposits and processing payments, should be in commercial banks, which would have access to government support. These banks should be prohibited from engaging in proprietary trading.

It might not be immediately evident to those who have not followed recent financial history why prohibiting commercial banks from engaging in proprietary trading could be seen as essentially banning investment banking in a commercial bank. Since when have investment banking and proprietary trading been the same thing? Answer: since roughly 50 years ago. Prior to the 1960s, commercial banking consisted primarily of the "utility" services noted by King, while investment banks underwrote sales of stock or bonds and offered advice on mergers and other transactions. With the increasing use of computer technology starting in the 1960s, however, and a revolution in financial economics thereafter (including the development by Fischer Black and Myron Scholes of the Black-Scholes option pricing model in 1973), proprietary trading became increasingly important to investment banks' bottom line. Proprietary trading is now the most lucrative investment banking business, and it is a mainstay of the largest commercial and combined commercial-investment banks (such as JPMorgan Chase) as well. Driving a wedge between traditional banking services and proprietary trading would thus force banks to choose between commercial banking (as J.P. Morgan did in the 1930s) and investment banking (the direction taken by Morgan Stanley, a J.P. Morgan spin-off).[14]

It is not difficult to see why the administration chafed at the Brandeisian approaches. With Geithner—who is so steeped in, committed to, and responsible for the 2008 bailouts—in a position to shape and promote the legislation, a more corporatist approach was inevitable—particularly given President Obama's confidence in Geithner.

Despite its hostility, the Obama administration was forced to make three concessions to the Brandeisians. The first and most important is the Volcker Rule, which is a version of Mervyn King's distinction between utility services and proprietary trading. In 2009, when Paul Volcker began advocating that Congress ban proprietary trading in commercial banks and forbid them from owning hedge funds or private equity funds, no one in the Obama administration was listening, as we saw in Chapter 3. Geithner and his staff at Treasury have never warmed to the concept, but it became part of Dodd-Frank as a result of perceived political imperatives.

As enacted, the Volcker Rule states that commercial banks cannot engage in proprietary trading, and that they cannot "acquire or retain any equity, partnership or other ownership interest in or sponsor a hedge fund or a private equity fund." The definition of commercial bank ("banking entity," in the jargon of the Act) covers not just an entity that does commercial banking, but any corporate structure that includes such an entity anywhere in its web of affiliates. Thus far, the Rule sounds quite similar to Volcker's conception. But slippage in both of its parts—due to the malleability of the term *proprietary trading* and a large exception to the ban on hedge fund and equity fund ownership—may give it a very different effect in practice.[15]

The definition of proprietary trading seems quite broad at first glance. The only exclusions are a series of innocuous-sounding activities such as trading in U.S. and agency obligations (such as Treasury bills), market making (that is, agreeing to buy or sell if someone else in the marketplace is looking for someone to take the other side of a transaction), hedging, and transactions made for customers. But these exclusions invite a great deal of manipulation. Just what constitutes a trade for the benefit of a customer will often be unclear, for instance, and the line between market making and trading for the bank's own account is equally slippery. Creative interpretation of proprietary and nonproprietary trading will permit a great deal of banks' current trading to continue. Even before the Act was signed into law, for instance, the *Wall Street Journal* reported that "banks are scrambling to find new positions for star proprietary traders, who basically trade company money in hopes of fattening bank profits and their own paychecks." Citigroup's likely strategy, according to the article, is "moving roughly two dozen proprietary traders onto desks that trade with company clients," where they can conduct essentially the same business as before so long as the trades can be characterized as requested by a client. As Janet Tavakoli, a leading derivatives trader, told the *New York Times*: "You can use client activity as a cover for basically anything you are doing.[16]

The principal escape hatch from the second part of the Volcker Rule is built right into the Act itself. A bank's investments in hedge funds and equity funds are defined as "de minimis" and excluded from the ban so long as the bank does not own more than 3 percent of any fund and its total interest does not exceed 3 percent of the value of the bank's core capital. (The technical term is Tier 1 capital, a yardstick that was itself a late concession to banks, replacing "tangible equity," a much narrower subset of a bank's core capital.) Most commercial banks will be able to fit within the 3 percent limitation without any significant shedding of assets.

The watering down of the Volcker Rule does not mean that the restriction will not have any bite—just that its implications may be quite different than Volcker himself intended. The banks for which the Volcker Rule poses the most immediate dilemma are Goldman Sachs and Morgan Stanley, the two investment banks that became bank holding companies in fall 2008 at the prodding of the Federal Reserve so that they would have access to full Fed borrowing privileges during the worst of the crisis. Both banks' investments in hedge and equity funds far exceed the 3 percent thresholds. Their predicament was an unintended—though anticipated—consequence of the Volcker Rule, since they aren't really commercial banks at all.

Some observers predicted that Goldman would give up its holding company status in order to escape the Volcker Rule. (If Goldman were not a bank holding company, it would not qualify as a "banking entity" for the purposes of the Volcker Rule, since it does not actually have any significant commercial banking operations.) Goldman's initial response, however, like Morgan Stanley's, was to begin shedding some of its proprietary trading operations. It is quite unlikely that either bank will meaningfully shrink in size as a result, however. A story focusing on negotiations by Morgan Stanley to reduce its stake in a hedge fund called Front-Point Partners, for instance, reported that "the Volcker Rule isn't the main reason Morgan Stanley is eager to shrink its stake." The more immediate concern was that "the business . . . hasn't proved as lucrative as expected."[17]

The second concession to the Brandeisians, which bears a family resemblance to the Volcker Rule, is the remains of the amendment introduced by Senator Blanche Lincoln. In its original conception, the Lincoln amendment would have prohibited any swaps trading within a commercial bank or a holding company that included a commercial bank. Senator Lincoln's particular concern was that banks, whose access to capital is subsidized by the government through deposit insurance and the right to borrow from the Fed, be prevented from gambling with the government's money through derivatives speculation. In its most sweeping version, her amendment not only would have prevented the commercial banking subsidiary in a bank holding company structure from dealing in derivatives; it would have excluded all of the other subsidiaries from the derivatives business as well.

As actually enacted, the limitation is less stringent. Although a commercial bank cannot itself deal in swaps, it can set up a separate subsidiary for derivatives trading. The precise mechanics of the rule, which experts refer to as the "swaps pushout" provision, are somewhat more subtle than I have suggested. The rule doesn't actually forbid banks from dealing in derivatives; it says that derivatives dealers are not entitled to certain forms of Federal Reserve funding. If there were no carve-out from this ban, banks and their affiliates would steer clear of derivatives, because they can't afford to lose access to Fed financing. But the rule says that a bank will not lose its funding if swaps trading is conducted by a separate affiliate rather than the bank—this is the "swaps pushout." Thus, the provision wouldn't stop a large bank holding company like Citigroup from trading in derivatives; Citigroup would simply need to hive off any derivatives operations that are currently conducted in its bank subsidiaries.

The banks themselves don't like the rule, because it may make their derivatives operations more costly. (This is because the derivatives affiliates will be subject to separate capital requirements, which is likely to decrease their overall profitability.) Despite the banks' objections, the policy basis for the rule is sound: There is no good reason for letting Citigroup or other large banks use the government-subsidized financing of a commercial bank affiliate to finance derivatives operations. But because the large banks can still conduct derivatives operations, the new rule will not force them to downsize.

The final concessions to the Brandeisians are nods in the direction of Simon Johnson's call for direct limits on the size of both banks and other systemically important financial institutions. Dodd-Frank states that no acquisition will be permitted if the acquiring institution has more than a 10 percent share of the overall liabilities of the financial services industry. If this concentration limit were an absolute ban, it might act as a significant curb on the growth of the largest financial institutions. It wouldn't force any of the big institutions to scale down, and they could still expand through internal growth. But the 10 percent rule would remove their ability to grow through acquisition, which—from John D. Rockefeller and Cornelius Vanderbilt a century ago to Citigroup and AIG in the 1980s and 1990s—has always been the principal path to behemoth status.[18]

But the 10 percent concentration limit has a large exception. The limit is waived if the systemically important institution will be acquiring a bank that is in default or in danger of default or if the Federal Deposit Insurance Corporation (FDIC) is involved in the transaction. With banks and other financial institutions, default acquisitions are where much of the action is. (And this tradition will be expanded much further by the new resolution regime, as we will see in Chapter 7.) The 10 percent limit would not have stopped either JPMorgan Chase's acquisition of Washington Mutual or the Wells Fargo purchase of Wachovia during the recent crisis.

In addition to the Brandeisian concessions we have discussed, the legislation also invites regulators to take extraordinary steps if there is a "grave threat" to financial stability. Under one of these provisions, the Fed can limit a firm's ability to merge with or acquire another company, restrict or forbid it from offering a particular financial product, force it "to terminate one or more activities," and even force it to sell off parts of its business, if two-thirds of the Financial Stability Oversight Council agrees.[19] But it is unlikely that these powers will be used under any realistically foreseeable circumstances. More likely they will function as a threat, as a stick in the Fed's partnership with Citigroup and other systemically important enterprises.

What Do the Brandeisian Concessions Mean?

The concessions the administration made to the Brandeisian perspective in order to secure passage of the Dodd–Frank Act are not irrelevant or unimportant. The Volcker Rule introduces complications for the largest banks and bank holding companies, as is already evident in the scurrying around by Goldman Sachs, Morgan Stanley, and other banks to reconfigure their proprietary trading operations. The concentration limit sweeps broadly enough that it will surely interfere with some acquisitions that the largest financial institutions would otherwise make. But there is no reason to believe that the largest financial institutions will start melting away.

The largest financial institutions can be sure that Dodd-Frank will not interfere with their dominance for another reason as well: To an extraordinary extent, the details of the legislation will be determined by banking regulators. Regulators are the ones who will decide just how tough the new capital rules for systemically important financial institutions should be, and how the Volcker Rule is applied. Regulators also will determine how the Collins amendment limitations on leverage apply to nonbank financial institutions. And many of these rules may not come fully into effect for two or three years.

Because they depend so heavily on regulatory discretion, the concessions to the Brandeisians aren't likely to shrink the largest financial institutions in any significant way. Instead, they will reinforce the partnership between regulators and the largest institutions. A new provision that authorizes bank regulators to prohibit forms of executive compensation they deem to be too risky may well have a similar effect. Thanks to Dodd-Frank, the Treasury secretary and other bank regulators now have new sticks they can use in their dealings with Wall Street.[20]

Even if regulators use their leverage to tamp down risk taking and reduce the likelihood that systemically important institutions will fail, the government's partnership with these institutions has two very troublesome implications. The first we have already seen: The companies that are cordoned off as systemically important distort the credit markets, as a result of the Fannie Mae effect. Because these institutions can raise capital more cheaply than financial institutions that do not enjoy implicit government protection, they have a competitive advantage over smaller institutions. This may dampen innovation in the financial system and lead to inefficient allocation of credit to nonfinancial businesses.

The second concern is that regulators will use their partnership with the largest financial institutions as a channel for political rather than financial considerations. The Obama administration's handling of the Chrysler bailout foreshadowed this possibility. As we saw in Chapter 2, the government structured the transaction to give Fiat a significantly larger ownership stake if it rolls out an energy-efficient car in the United States, thus promoting one of the administration's signature political objectives. The Dodd-Frank Act not only invites this mixing of political and economic objectives; it positively encourages it, in ways both direct and more subtle.

Office of Minority and Women Inclusion

Buried deep in the heart of the Dodd-Frank Act is a provision that epitomizes the new government-bank partnership in American financial regulation. This provision instructs every financial regulator to establish an Office of Minority and Women Inclusion. The Federal Reserve must therefore establish such an office, as must the Department of the Treasury, the SEC, the CFTC, and every other financial regulator. In each agency, the new office is instructed to police all the financial services regulators to make sure that the agencies hire adequate numbers of women and minorities. This in itself is a sweeping mandate, but a defensible and potentially desirable one. Yet the offices' mandate goes even further. They are charged with policing every entity that enters into any kind of contract with a financial services regulator as well. Because every large bank contracts with the government in one way or another—to administer the assets of the Troubled Asset Relief Program (TARP) fund, for instance, or to help run auctions of government securities—the provision is tantamount to subjecting every systemically important institution (and many other companies as well) to the oversight of one or more Offices of Minority and Women Inclusion.

Because the entire purpose of each Office of Minority and Women Inclusion is to police diversity, it can be expected to begin counting the number of minority and women executives and directors at the systemically important financial firms. By threatening to cancel contracts, an Office of Minority and Women Inclusion could force boards to select executives based on their demographics—at least if the new offices are not struck down as unconstitutional by the current Supreme Court.

Diversity is an enormously important issue. But pursuing this objective through a partnership between government and private firms is a dangerous strategy that could further inject political factors into the governance and operations of the largest financial institutions.

Institutionalizing the Government-Bank Partnership

The Dodd-Frank Act incorporates political policy into bank regulation in much more pervasive ways as well. Perhaps most important and least discussed in this regard is the extensive new authority given by the new legislation to the Department of the Treasury, the most directly political of the financial regulators. The secretary of the Treasury is made first among equals on the new Financial Stability Oversight Council, and Treasury also runs a major new research organization, the Office of Financial Research, authorized by Dodd-Frank. Much more than truly independent agencies like the Fed and the SEC, the Treasury is beholden to the executive branch and will bring the President's political concerns to bear in its oversight of the largest banks, particularly in or near election years. As a result, the Dodd-Frank Act virtually ensures that the government will lean on the systemically important financial institutions, injecting political calculations into their business operations.

More generally, the Dodd-Frank Act invites the government to channel political policy through the big financial institutions by giving regulators sweeping discretion in the enforcement of each of the provisions we have been discussing. Suppose, for instance, that regulators are determining whether a group of Citigroup bankers are engaged in proprietary trading at a time when the government is unhappy with the big oil companies, or with weapons manufacturers. It is not hard to imagine Citigroup's directors concluding that they had better limit Citigroup's financing of the disfavored industry if they wish to get sympathetic treatment as regulators decide whether the bank is in compliance with the Volcker Rule. Many other provisions will give regulators similar leverage in their partnership with the largest financial institutions.

A Happier Story?

Perhaps I seem too pessimistic. I can imagine a more optimistic story about the likely effect of the Dodd-Frank Act, and some readers may be imagining such stories, too, even at this point in our discussion. Suppose that the Fed, the Treasury, the new Council, and other regulators enforce the new Dodd-Frank regulations vigorously, as certainly is possible while memories of the financial crisis are still fresh. By imposing strict capital requirements on the largest financial institutions, regulators may reduce the risk of a Fannie Mae effect that crowds out smaller competitors. And if they enforce the Volcker Rule with gusto, the largest banks might naturally simplify and shrink, at least a little. And if nearly all swaps migrate to clearinghouses and exchanges, this could give smaller financial institutions a chance to grab a piece of the derivatives business, much as deposit insurance gave small banks a chance to attract deposits after the New Deal. The result might be more competition on Wall Street, and less domination by the largest banks.

This is possible in theory, but in reality it simply won't happen. As we discussed earlier, it will be almost impossible for regulators to impose capital standards strict enough to eliminate the advantages of the systemically important firms. The firms can plausibly argue that strict standards would cripple them and force them to move more of their operations overseas; they also can argue that higher capital standards will dampen big banks' lending to American businesses.

The Volcker Rule is a similar story. It was never a particularly compelling regulatory strategy, because proprietary trading is too closely intertwined with other functions. And foreign regulators are highly unlikely to impose similar restrictions. Most other countries did not follow the United States' lead in separating commercial from investment banking during the Depression, so they have long histories of combining the two, and little incentive to change now. As a result, the United States' systemically important financial institutions can argue that they will be forced to move their proprietary operations overseas if regulators enforce the Volcker Rule too strictly.

There is little evidence that the current administration is interested in downsizing the largest financial institutions. In an important speech given the month after Dodd-Frank was enacted, for instance, Secretary Geithner talked about the new capital standards at length in his discussion of the "new rules to constrain risk taking by—and leverage in—the largest global financial institutions," but completely ignored the Volcker Rule and other Brandeisian concessions.[21] As a result, it is much more likely that the big banks and other dominant financial institutions will stay big. Rather than forcing them to downsize or to genuinely relinquish their stranglehold on derivatives and other financial innovations, regulators will use their new powers under Dodd-Frank as bargaining chips in their partnership with the systemically important firms.

Repo Land Mine

There is one more danger—of a very different sort—in the regulatory structure as it stands after Dodd-Frank. As we have seen, lawmakers tried to limit the systemic risk posed by the largest financial institutions by singling them out and subjecting them to higher capital standards. The legislation also introduces at least limited leverage restrictions. But lawmakers left an important source of risk essentially untouched: investment banks' reliance on very short-term repo financing.

Both Bear Stearns and Lehman Brothers saw their liquidity—that is, their access to sufficient cash to finance operations—evaporate almost instantly when their repo creditors refused to roll over their financing. In a repo financing, a borrower like Bear Stearns or Lehman sells securities (anything from Treasury bills to mortgage-backed securities) to the lender, and at the same time agrees to buy them back at a higher price. The difference between the prices is like interest on a loan. Repo transactions are generally short-term in nature, in part because many of the lenders—the repo buyers—are money market funds that are not permitted to hold long-term obligations. During the crisis, the repos often lasted for only 24 hours. This meant that Bear, Lehman, and other borrowers had to renew the loans every day, and could almost instantly lose their access to funds.

Economist Gary Gorton compares the effect of jitters in the repo market to the bank runs that plagued American finance prior to the New Deal legislation that created deposit insurance. Just as solvent commercial banks could fail in the face of massive withdrawals by panicked depositors, a solvent financial institution that depends on repo financing can fail if repo buyers lose confidence in the repo market. Gorton has suggested that the government should address the problem of repo runs in the same way it solved deposit runs: through government guarantees. The cost of this solution would be enormous, and Gorton seems to assume that it is important to ensure that the financial markets in general, and the repo market in particular, remain as large as they were before the crisis.[22]

More limited solutions—such as requiring that repos last longer than a day or imposing a liquidity tax on the use of short-term debt— would be more realistic. Altering the treatment of derivatives in bankruptcy, a possibility I discuss in Chapter 9, might dampen somewhat investment banks' incentive to rely as heavily on repo financing as they came to do prior to the crisis.

But Dodd-Frank ignores the repo issue almost completely. The only recognition of the dangerous fragility of repo financing is found in provisions authorizing the Fed to limit the amount of short-term debt a systemically important firm is permitted to have, and calling for yet another study—in this case, of the effects of short-term financing.[23] The Fed's funding authority appears to extend to repos, which suggests that the only option in the event of problems may be more bailouts. The failure to address the risk that large nonbank financial institutions could suddenly lose their financing is yet another reason why the legislation's resolution provisions are so important. We consider these provisions in detail in Chapters 7 and 8. But before turning to resolution, we should consider the most unlikely feature of the new legislation: the new Consumer Financial Protection Bureau.

Chapter 6

Unsafe at Any Rate

According to the words of an old Biblical proverb, "The stone that the builders rejected has become the cornerstone."[1] The theme is that of an unexpected triumph. If any portion of the Dodd-Frank Act can be said to fit this theme, it is the new Consumer Financial Protection Bureau. Washington insiders repeatedly predicted its demise, or at least that it would be weakened to the point of irrelevance. At a bipartisan task force meeting I attended in January 2010, for instance, the legislative expert pointed out that President Obama hadn't mentioned the Bureau (which was still envisioned as an agency) in a speech he'd just given on the reforms, which the expert took as a signal that the administration was willing to abandon it. But the Bureau survived, with more clout and independence than almost anyone imagined possible.

Prior to the Dodd-Frank Act, consumer protection for mortgage, credit card, and other financial concerns was scattered through a maze of agencies and other enforcers. Principal responsibility was vested in the Federal Reserve, but the Federal Trade Commission (FTC) also had extensive enforcement powers, and the Comptroller of the Currency and other regulators also had roles. The problem wasn't that too many cooks spoiled the broth; it was that none of the cooks seemed to be in the kitchen. As complaints about predatory lending in the subprime mortgage markets increased in the early 2000s, the Federal Reserve dithered, barely responding at all as the decade wore on. Barney Frank was so disgusted with the Fed's inaction that he threatened to push for Congress to bypass the Fed and legislate directly. Even Ben Bernanke has subsequently conceded that the Fed fell down on the job, though he promised it would do better next time.

In a sense the Fed will, since the new Consumer Bureau is technically a part of the Fed. But it is so independent, and has such significant powers, that it might as well be entirely on its own. Physically, in fact, it is: The new Bureau will be housed in its own building, apart from the Fed.

The Consumer Bureau is the one of the rarest of all Washington creations. It is a legislative innovation that was conceived by a leading scholar, and unlike the overwhelming majority of scholarly ideas, has actually come to fruition. As we saw in Chapter 3, Harvard Law Professor Elizabeth Warren outlined the vision in a short 2007 article, followed by a more elaborate analysis in a co-authored article the following year.[2] With a few exceptions, the legislative blueprint for the new Consumer Bureau reads as if it came straight from these two articles, as in many respects it did.[3]

Basic Framework

Here, in summary form, are some of the key features we will be considering:

- Bureau of the Federal Reserve.
- Director is appointed by President with consent of Senate.
  - Five-year term, removable only for cause.
  - Voting member of Financial Stability Oversight Council.

- Scope: mortgages, credit cards, and other aspects of consumer finance.
- Broad powers:
  - Rules reviewable only for systemic risk concerns.
- Funding: 10 to 12 percent of Federal Reserve budget.
  - Current estimate: $500 million.

As I have already noted, the Consumer Financial Protection Bureau is nominally part of the Federal Reserve. But the Fed will have almost no real control over the Bureau's day-to-day operations or its regulatory oversight.

The director of the Bureau is appointed by the President, with the advice and consent of the Senate, just like other agency heads. The director serves a five-year term, and neither the President, the Fed, nor anyone else has the power to remove the director except in the event of misbehavior.

The core of the Bureau's regulatory portfolio is credit cards and mortgages, although its authority extends to a wide variety of other consumer financial transactions as well, including pawn shop and pay-day loan operations. Within these areas, the Bureau has the full pan-oply of regulatory powers at its disposal. Subject to a few important exceptions I discuss later in the chapter, the Bureau can promulgate new rules, it can hold hearings, and it can litigate to protect consum-ers' interests.

In theory, the other financial regulators have some authority to police the Bureau's rule making. But in order to set aside a rule put in place by the Bureau, two-thirds of the voting members of the Financial Stability Oversight Council must agree that the rule threatens the banking system or the nation's financial stability.

The one area where the Bureau does depend on the Fed to some extent is for its funding. The Bureau will be funded from the Fed's gen-eral appropriation. The Fed is instructed to direct up to 10 percent of its funds to the Bureau in 2011, 11 percent in 2012, and 12 percent in 2013 and thereafter. These percentages are a ceiling, rather than a floor. But the Fed surely will provide most or all of this funding for the Bureau, at least in the beginning. Just to make sure the Bureau is well funded, the new legislation authorizes its director to ask Congress for an additional $200 million per year if the director concludes that the Bureau does not have enough funding.

Because the Consumer Bureau began with Elizabeth Warren, we will, too. After putting Warren's career in historical context, we will consider the structure and powers of the new Bureau, how it will function in practice, and its potential consequences. We also will consider President Obama's decision to appoint Warren as de facto head of the new Bureau without going through the normal nomination process, which injected a great deal of uncertainty into the Bureau's launch. More than any other part of the Dodd-Frank Act, the new Consumer Bureau could become a meaningful counterweight to the systemically important banks we considered in the preceding chapter.

Who Is Elizabeth Warren?

It may seem altogether unnecessary to ask the question, "Who is Elizabeth Warren?" By far the best-known law professor in the country, Warren would rank high on any current list of American public figures. When I first wrote these words, a YouTube video promoting Warren's nomination was making the rounds. There were cartoons showing Warren as a sheriff policing the wilds of Wall Street, and stories about her in the newspapers and Web media daily. Unknown she is not.

Yet the historical context for Warren's recent burst to prominence will be unfamiliar to all but a few. As a bankruptcy scholar, Warren has followed a course that interestingly echoes the career of William O. Douglas, the Yale Law School professor who became head of the Securities and Exchange Commission (SEC) and then Supreme Court justice for more than 30 years, and who may have declined an offer to be Franklin Roosevelt's running mate in 1944. A decade ago, a scholar wrote:

> Foremost among the current progressives is Elizabeth Warren. Like Douglas, Warren decries the dearth of empirical data and insists on the need both to fill this gap and to use empirical

work to inform an agenda for constructive change. In words that echo Douglas's approach, she proclaims that "a debate without data is a useless excursion, a trip from nowhere to nowhere."[4]

This quotation (with which I am quite familiar, having written it) identifies the central emphasis of Warren's scholarly work. Much like Douglas, who conducted extensive empirical studies of bankruptcy before entering public life, Warren staked her career on the relentless collection and analysis of data.

Although empirical analysis is now standard fare in legal scholarship (as it was for a time in Douglas's era), it was relatively uncommon in the early 1980s when Warren and two co-authors—Teresa Sullivan and Jay Westbrook—began their first major study of consumer bankruptcy: *As We Forgive Our Debtors*, published in 1989. Based on their analysis of 1,547 cases filed in 10 courts in Texas, Pennsylvania, and Illinois, they found that Americans who file for bankruptcy have more debt and less income than those who don't; and, more surprisingly, that debtors do not hail disproportionately from low-pay, low-prestige occupations. Warren and her co-authors pursued these findings still further in an even larger study published as *The Fragile Middle Class* in 2000. Among other things, they found that the best predictors of the likelihood that a consumer will file for bankruptcy include loss of a job, divorce, and health problems.[5]

Warren's first best seller was *The Two-Income Trap*, which she co-authored with her daughter. The book chronicled the changes in living, housing, and other expenses from 1970 to 2000, relying on both her bankruptcy data and other sources of data, and concluded that many American couples need two jobs to hang on to their perch in the middle class. They are one crisis away from disaster. The book attracted the attention of John Edwards during his 2004 presidential campaign, and made the rounds of Washington policy circles.[6]

The other hallmark of Warren's career, in addition to statistics and data collection, is advocacy. The stances with which Warren is identified were evident from her earliest work. One of her first articles challenged an academic study funded by credit card companies that concluded many consumer debtors who filed for bankruptcy were capable of repaying some of what they owed. The study, she and her two co-authors argued, "lacks crucial expertise, is designed incorrectly, asks a series of inartful questions, gathers its data improperly, misanalyzes the statistical data and draws erroneous and biased inferences from the data analysis." Her books and subsequent articles remained harshly critical of lenders, especially credit card banks, and came to the defense of consumer debtors.[7]

While Warren had clearly defined views from the beginning, her public embrace of the advocate's role came as a result of her work on the National Bankruptcy Review Commission, a commission set up by Congress in 1994 to study American bankruptcy and devise proposals for reform. Representatives of the consumer credit industry were a frequent presence at the Commission's meetings and hearings. They were not pleased with the Commission's consumer bankruptcy recommendations, which were much closer to Warren's views than the creditors'. The lenders had argued, for instance, for restricting a debtor's choice whether to file under Chapter 7, which gives the debtor an immediate discharge from debts, rather than under Chapter 13, in which the debtor agrees to repay some of what is owed under a three- to five-year repayment plan. The Commission rejected these arguments, defending debtors' unfettered choice. To defuse the Commission's findings, the consumer credit industry persuaded Congress to introduce bankruptcy reforms more to their liking shortly before the Commission transmitted its final report to Congress in early 1997.

In the clash over the proposed legislation, which eventually led to major bankruptcy reform in 2005 (and a new means test that bans consumer debtors from Chapter 7 under some circumstances), Elizabeth Warren emerged as consumer debtors' preeminent defender. During the eight years of debate, Warren testified against the bill and frequented the op-ed pages. Drawing on the data from her studies, which showed that a large and growing percentage of bankruptcy debtors were women, she condemned the proposed legislation as antiwomen, since it would make bankruptcy more costly and difficult. A scholarly article that surveyed bankruptcy scholars' media involvement during the legislative debates found dozens of stories quoting Warren; no one else even came close. (George Mason bankruptcy scholar Todd Zywicki, one of the few scholars who defended the credit card companies and the legislation, was a distant second.)[8]

This was the context in which Elizabeth Warren published her now-famous 2007 article, "Unsafe at Any Rate." Americans of a certain age will immediately recognize the article's title as a reference to *Unsafe at Any Speed*, the famous 1965 book by Ralph Nader, Warren's predecessor as the nation's leading consumer advocate. Much as Nader's book and his accompanying campaign lambasted General Motors for building cars that put consumers at unnecessary risk, Warren's article condemned the "tricks and traps" used by credit card companies to profit at consumers' expense.[9]

Toasters and Credit Cards

The article's central motif was the contrast between toasters, which are effectively regulated, and consumer finance, which isn't. "It is impossible to buy a toaster that has a one-in-five chance of bursting into flames and burning down your house," Warren began. "But it is possible to refinance an existing home with a mortgage that has the same one-in-five chance of putting the family out on the street—and the mortgage won't even carry a disclosure of that fact to the homeowner. Similarly," she continued, "it's impossible to change the price on a toaster once it has been purchased. But long after the papers have been signed, it is possible to triple the price of the credit used to finance the purchase of that appliance." Why, Warren asked, are customers protected when they buy toasters, but not "when they sign up for routine financial products like mortgages and credit cards?"[10]

The answer, Warren argued, is that consumer goods are carefully regulated by the Consumer Product Safety Commission, whereas mortgages and credit cards "are regulated by a tattered patchwork of federal and state laws that have failed to adapt to changing markets." The logical solution, she contended, was to establish a new regulator with the authority to provide the same kind of protection regarding mortgages and credit cards that consumers have with toasters and other appliances.

Such an agency "would promote the benefits of free markets by assuring that consumers can enter credit markets with confidence that the products they purchase meet minimum safety standards."[11]

The following year, Warren published a more detailed and scholarly (with many more footnotes, in other words) version of her proposal with another law professor, Oren Bar-Gill of New York University. In the more recent article, Warren and Bar-Gill surveyed a wide range of data about credit card use. Drawing on recent work in behavioral economics—which explores cognitive biases that can systemically distort consumers' decision making—they argued that new disclosure requirements would not be sufficient to protect consumers. Because consumers often underestimate the likelihood they will miss future payments, for instance, simply requiring lenders to disclose the potential fees is not enough. Nor could existing regulators adequately champion consumers' interests. Because of its concern for the financial health of banks, which may benefit from practices that gouge consumers, the Federal Reserve faced an intractable conflict of interest; and the other regulators with a stake in consumer regulation had similar conflicts, and only limited authority, or were spread too thin. Financial institutions also were able to play one regulator off another, due to the fragmentation of banking regulation among state and federal regulators. Consumers needed a new, unconflicted regulator to protect their interests.[12]

With the enactment of the Dodd-Frank Act, this is precisely what they got.

The New Consumer Bureau

Although it is part of the Federal Reserve—nominally, at least—the Consumer Financial Protection Bureau is essentially an independent executive agency. As with an independent agency, the director is nominated by the President, with the "advice and consent" of the Senate, to serve a five-year term. Once appointed, the director cannot be removed, absent misbehavior, before the end of the term. The director also is a member of the new Financial Stability Oversight Council.[13]

The Consumer Bureau's principal focus is the issues we have been discussing, mortgages and credit cards, but its scope is technically somewhat broader than this (and is limited in several respects as well). The Bureau has authority over any "covered person" that offers or provides a "consumer financial product or service." Consumer financial product or service includes, among other things, extending credit and servicing loans, making or brokering leases on real estate, and providing financial advisory services to consumers. A number of industries are excluded from the Bureau's oversight—including insurance, tax preparers, and employee benefit plans. The most serious of the exclusions is auto lending; although auto loans are a major financial concern for many consumers, the auto industry persuaded Congress to exclude these loans from Bureau oversight. But anyone who offers or provides a "consumer financial product or service," and isn't excluded, answers to the new Bureau. This most definitely includes mortgage providers and credit card companies, as well as pawn shops and payday lenders.[14]

To make way for the new Bureau, the legislation will transfer a wide range of powers from pre-Dodd-Frank regulators to the new consumer champion. The Act takes away all of the Federal Reserve's consumer protection responsibility, as well as all of the responsibilities of a variety of other regulators and some of the prior authority of the Federal Trade Commission.[15]

Equally important, the legislation guarantees funding commensurate with the Consumer Bureau's scope of authority, at least initially. The Federal Reserve is instructed to appropriate up to 10 percent of its funding to the Consumer Bureau in 2011, up to 11 percent for 2011, and up to 12 percent for 2013 and thereafter—the appropriation would be roughly $500 million in the first year. And if the director concludes that the Bureau is underfunded and prepares a report for the President, Senate, and House to this effect, the Bureau is guaranteed an additional $200 million per year from 2010 to 2014.[16]

Of particular note for legislation that singles out the largest financial institutions for special treatment, the Dodd-Frank Act gives the new Bureau exclusive regulatory authority on consumer protection issues over financial institutions with more than $10 billion in assets, and much less authority with smaller banks. The divergence is starkest with enforcement. While the Bureau has strong enforcement powers with respect to large financial institutions, it cannot enforce against small ones. The distinction was a compromise for the benefit of community banks, and could noticeably undermine the Bureau's scope. But its effect is to focus the Bureau's attention on the same banks that are singled out elsewhere in the legislation.[17]

As I have already hinted, the Consumer Bureau's powers are quite broad. It has rule-making authority—which means that it has the authority to promulgate new rules under the consumer protection laws that it has responsibility for. A key question prior to the final enactment of Dodd-Frank was whether the Federal Reserve or other bank regulators would have the power to thwart the implementation of a rule proposed by the Consumer Bureau. Except under the most extraordinary circumstances, they won't. Only if two-thirds of the new Financial Stability Oversight Council conclude that it would "put the safety and soundness of the U.S. banking system or the stability of the financial system" at risk can a rule prescribed by the Consumer Bureau be set aside.[18]

In addition to its rule-making power, the Consumer Bureau has all of the other regulatory powers of a major financial regulator. It can hold hearings, and it can bring civil litigation to enforce the consumer laws. These powers leave little doubt that the Consumer Bureau is a force to be reckoned with.[19]

Along with its general regulatory powers, the Dodd-Frank Act also authorizes the Consumer Bureau to provide "model forms" for consumer loans. The predecessor of this provision was a source of considerable controversy during the legislative debates. In the original draft of the legislation, the consumer regulator would have been authorized to require that mortgage providers and credit card companies provide "plain-vanilla" loan agreements as an option for consumers. This proposal drew heated opposition from the consumer credit industry, and was seriously weakened. The provision that was enacted authorizes the Consumer Bureau to draft model forms. But the provision does not give the Bureau the power to force lenders to offer agreements based on these forms.[20]

Another important limitation on the Consumer Bureau's authority concerns interest rates. Credit card companies can charge extraordinarily high interest rates in any state in the country, due to a 1978

Supreme Court decision (and a subsequent banking regulation on the same theme) holding that the interest rates are regulated by the state where the credit card bank is incorporated, not the state where the consumer lives. After this decision, the credit card banks all moved to the states with the weakest restrictions—primarily South Dakota and Delaware. A state like Wisconsin that has tough usury laws—that is, laws that prohibit high interest loans—therefore has little say about the interest rates its citizens will be charged. Many scholars (including this one) have advocated legislation to reverse this rule, and to allow each state to regulate the interest rates that apply to its citizens. The big consumer lenders are of course adamantly opposed. The Dodd-Frank Act sides with the lenders, stating: "No provision of this title shall be construed as conferring authority on the Bureau to establish a usury limit . . . unless explicitly authorized by law." Whether this provision would preclude measures that would have a similar effect, such as a regulation basing interest rates on the consumer's domicile rather than a credit card bank's state of incorporation, is, at the outset, anyone's guess.[21]

Mortgage Broker and Securitization Rules

While the Consumer Bureau is the center of consumer protection activity, the Dodd-Frank Act also includes several other reforms that should be seen as a supplemental part of the consumer protection package.

The first set of reforms focuses on mortgage originators—the mortgage brokers or other professionals who arrange mortgage financing. In response to widespread complaints that many mortgage brokers steered consumers to higher-priced mortgages and had a financial incentive to do so, the legislation makes it illegal for a mortgage originator to receive more for a higher-priced loan than a lower-priced one. The fee cannot depend in any way on the cost of the loan. The legislation also instructs the Federal Reserve to prescribe new regulations that prevent originators from steering consumers to loans they can't pay.[22]

The other set of reforms, which is not limited to consumer transactions, targets a defect in the process by which mortgages were sold and repackaged during the recent housing bubble—the process known as securitization. After banks or mortgage lenders make loans, they often quickly sell the loans, rather than holding the mortgages and collecting the payments as they would have done 30 or 40 years ago. The buyer of the mortgage is usually a special entity (the special purpose vehicle or special purpose entity) created by an investment bank. Simplifying slightly, the financing to purchase the mortgages comes from investors, who receive securities (which are usually divided into different tranches, with different levels of riskiness) issued by the special entity in return for their investment. When (or if) homeowners make payments on their mortgages, most of this money is used for the payments due on the investors' securities. Along the way, the investment bank takes a fee for arranging the securitization.

Although this process has many virtues, such as reducing the risk that banks face if they hold all the mortgages themselves, banks and mortgage lenders had very little incentive to carefully scrutinize their borrowers if they planned immediately to sell the mortgages to someone else. One study found that mortgages that had been securitized were 10 to 25 percent more likely to default than those the lender retained.[23]

The Dodd-Frank Act instructs the SEC and banking regulators to prescribe regulations that will require the securitizer—ordinarily, an investment bank—to retain at least 5 percent of the risk of the transaction. Regulators are invited to promulgate rules dividing the risk retention obligation between the securitizer and the originator in transactions in which unrelated entities perform the two roles. The rationale is that lenders are likely to be much more careful if they have a stake in the quality of the mortgage loans they make. The requirement will not apply to *qualified residential mortgages*—once that term is defined by the SEC and bank regulators.[24]

Both reforms are designed to reshape some of the perverse regulatory incentives that contributed to the financial crisis. The securitization problem almost certainly would have been addressed by market participants themselves, as the investment bank and the investors both have an interest in encouraging lenders to take a closer look at their borrowers, particularly now that the housing bubble has burst. But the pattern of mortgage brokers steering homeowners to high-cost loans might well have continued, since it benefited both the lenders and the brokers—at the expense of consumers.

Consequences: What to Expect from the New Bureau

The long-term significance of the Consumer Bureau will depend heavily on whether it quickly establishes itself as a significant regulatory player. The obvious historical analogy is the Securities and Exchange Commission. I will begin with the historical analogy and its implications, then turn to the likely effect of the Bureau on consumer credit markets.

The SEC was established in 1934 to police the stock and bond markets, largely with retail investors—that is, consumers—in mind. President Roosevelt had initially wanted to leave this task with the Federal Trade Commission, most of whose commissioners were staunch New Dealers. To defuse conservative opposition, the administration agreed to the creation of the SEC. Roosevelt then brought several commissioners over from the FTC to the new SEC, and appointed a very strong and surprising initial chairman: Joseph Kennedy. Kennedy immediately established the political heft of the SEC, and set a pattern of aggressive enforcement.[25]

Although Elizabeth Warren was far less of a surprise, since the Bureau was her vision, she will put the Bureau on the map in the same way as its New Deal predecessor. This does not guarantee that the Bureau will invariably remain a major regulatory presence filled with top-notch personnel, of course. The SEC stands as testimony to the ups and downs in the life of a regulatory agency: In the 1950s and again more recently, the SEC was dispirited and often ineffectual as a regulator. In each case, inadequate funding seems to have been a key part of the problem.

While the Consumer Bureau has been assured major funding for its launch, the guaranteed funding stops as of 2014. There no doubt will be times when the Federal Reserve will scale down its funding in the future, particularly given that the Bureau's mission and the Fed's are not altogether in sync.

But this is in the future. The Bureau has a high profile and highly motivated de facto head during its startup period, with a $500 million budget for effectuating her vision of a consumer credit market that more robustly protects ordinary Americans. What impact will this have?

Some of the Bureau's first steps are directed by the legislation itself, which instructs the Bureau to set up an office focusing on credit market risks to older consumers, and to establish offices near military bases. The Bureau surely will begin devising model forms, which are likely to be most influential while the Bureau's powers are at their peak, and will make aggressive use of its powers to hold hearings, investigate and require information from lenders, and bring civil lawsuits. The power to investigate and require data may be the most important power of all. As a scholar seeking data, Warren was not a welcome presence at the offices of the credit card banks. But now the banks are required to open their doors and answer questions about their business practices.

Two obvious questions regarding the Consumer Bureau are whether its oversight will stunt innovation and increase the cost (and decrease availability) of consumer credit. Warren has a ready response to the first of these concerns. "It is important to distinguish good innovation and bad innovation," she told Congress in 2009:

Figuring out one more trick that boosts company revenues while picking a customer's pocket is not good innovation. Again, the analogy to physical products is useful. The Consumer Product Safety Commission does not permit manufacturers to "innovate" by cutting down on insulation or removing shutoff switches. Safety is the baseline, so toaster manufacturers compete by coming up with better products at lower prices.[26]

The second issue, the possibility that new regulation will make credit cards and mortgages more expensive or harder to get, could involve more of a trade-off, as Warren has recognized in her writing. Speaking of interest rate regulation in her book *The Two-Income Trap*, for instance, Warren speculates that some "families with weaker credit histories or more modest incomes might find themselves limited to smaller homes, but they would also be far less likely to end up in a home that drove them into the bankruptcy courts." Similarly, if interest rates on credit cards were restricted, "banks would have far greater incentive to screen cardholders, offering only as much credit as each party could pay."[27]

As we have seen, the Consumer Bureau does not have the authority to limit interest rates. But greater enforcement and more careful investigation of lenders and their lending practices could have a similar effect, prompting lenders to restrict the access of lower-middle-class consumers to credit. If this tightening of credit discouraged consumers from borrowing more than they could repay, it would be a cost worth paying. If it simply constricted access, there would be more cause for concern.

For more affluent consumers, the most likely cost of more vigorous consumer protection may be the gradual disappearance of freebies like credit cards with no annual fee that earn frequent-flier miles and other perks. These perks are subsidized by the high interest rates and fees paid by consumers who are unable to pay off their balances each month.

We can't really know in advance whether these costs will materialize, of course. Moreover, the answer will depend on how the Consumer Bureau pursues its regulatory mandate, which will be different at different times in the Bureau's life. For now, the chief question is simply whether a new consumer champion is justified. Given the absence of meaningful protection before the crisis, the answer clearly is yes.

This doesn't mean that home buyers and consumers with large balances on their credit cards were all victims. Many who are in difficult straits now may bear responsibility for their predicaments. But there was no one effectively policing what Warren calls the "tricks and traps" of consumer lending.

What It Means for the
Government-Bank Partnership

I noted earlier that the Consumer Bureau's principal focus will be the lending practices of the largest banks, thanks to the community banks' success in persuading Congress to carve them out of the Bureau's regulatory mandate. This means—purely as an accident of the legislative process—that the Consumer Bureau will direct much of its attention to the same banks we discussed in Chapter 5.

The structure of the credit card market confirms the centrality of the systemically important banks to the Consumer Bureau's new mission. The top four banks by general credit card billings as of June 30, 2009, were Chase, with $165.87 billion outstanding; Bank of America, with $150.82 billion; Citi, with $102.54 billion; and American Express, with $78.16 billion. JPMorgan Chase, Bank of America, Citi, and American Express are all among the giant bank holding companies that automatically qualify for systemically important status under the Dodd-Frank Act.[28]

Like the Volcker Rule and the concentration limits we considered in Chapter 5, the Consumer Financial Protection Bureau runs counter to the Dodd-Frank Act's endorsement of the biggest financial institutions, and its expansion of too-big-to-fail status. The Bureau was not a concession by the administration in quite the same sense as the Volcker Rule, since the administration endorsed it very early on, at the urging of Larry Summers. But Timothy Geithner made little secret of his discomfort with the Consumer Bureau, and he worked to undercut it throughout the process.

With good reason. The Consumer Bureau won't function at all like the Volcker Rule. As we saw in Chapter 5, while the Volcker Rule purports to cut back on the scope and power of the giant banks, it actually will cement the partnership between the government and the largest banks. The Consumer Bureau will neither strengthen the banks' hand nor reinforce the government-bank partnership. Unlike any other part of the Dodd-Frank Act, the Consumer Bureau will serve as a counterweight. It will limit the kinds of strategies that the largest banks can use to make profits. It is possible, of course, that the Consumer

Bureau will be co-opted or ineffectual at times in the future. But its very purpose is to rein the banks in, rather than to simply enable them.

The awkward start of the Consumer Bureau may complicate its assertion of authority. Faced with the prospect that Elizabeth Warren could not be confirmed as director due to strident bank opposition, President Obama sidestepped the nomination process by naming Warren as his assistant and a special adviser to Treasury secretary Geithner for the new Bureau. Not only did this reinforce concerns about ad hoc circumvention of the rule of law, it also limits the initial scope of the Bureau in important respects. Because Warren is not technically director, she cannot participate on the Financial Stability Oversight Council, and lenders may balk at the initiatives she undertakes as not reflecting the decisions of an actual director. Warren also has appreciably less independence as a presidential assistant than a formal director would have. But even with these constraints, the Bureau is already a much more powerful advocate than consumers have had in the past.

Sixty-five years ago, during the New Deal, organized labor was thought by many to be a necessary counterweight to the largest industrial firms. In today's financial services industry, the focus has shifted to consumers and their new champion, the Consumer Financial Protection Bureau.

Chapter 7

Banking on the FDIC (Resolution Authority I)

Whed Harvard Business School Professor David Moss testified at a congressional hearing in October 2009, he argued that there are three possible options for resolving the financial distress of the largest financial institutions: bankruptcy, bailouts, and an administrative resolution process. "The good news," Moss said, is that the Federal Deposit Insurance Corporation (FDIC) has had resolution authority for years with respect to commercial banks, and "it has worked well. . . . What is needed now," he concluded, "is a comparable resolution process for all [systemically important financial institutions], whether they are banks, bank holding companies, or other financial institutions. We need a resolution process that works, so regulators don't have to be afraid to let [them] fail."[1]

The Obama administration made the same argument: Their framework for administrative resolution of large financial institutions didn't "institutionalize bailouts," as critics complained; it would provide the benefits of bankruptcy without the uncertainty. The model, they too argued, is the FDIC's handling of ordinary bank failures. Assistant Treasury Secretary Michael Barr, Timothy Geithner's point person for the legislation, put it this way: "Our proposal does little more than apply to [systemically important financial institutions] the same model that Congress has developed, that the FDIC has executed, and that courts have respected, over the course of more than three-quarters of a century."[2]

The claim is simple and alluring. The FDIC does a great job handling the failures of small and medium-sized banks, the reasoning goes. But the FDIC has authority only over depositary bank subsidiaries. It doesn't have the power to resolve the financial distress of bank holding companies, the affiliates of a depositary bank, or other kinds of financial institutions. Extending the FDIC's power to large financial institutions would fill the gap; it's the perfect alternative to the bailouts of 2008.

Many thoughtful observers were persuaded by the analogy, and are enthusiastic advocates for the new resolution regime. Is the FDIC analogy compelling? To answer this question, we need to examine the key unstated assumptions underlying it: that the FDIC is indeed extremely successful in its current resolution efforts; that the FDIC will have the same role in the new resolution regime as it has with ordinary banks; and that the strategies the FDIC uses for handling small and medium-sized bank failures will be effective when a gigantic firm fails.

As you may have guessed, our topic in this chapter is the FDIC analogy that was used to sell the new resolution regime. In Chapter 8, we will consider the specific details of the new resolution regime in much more detail, focusing in particular on the question whether it will discourage bailouts when systemically important firms fail in the future.

Does the FDIC Play the Same Role in Both Regimes?

It may be useful to begin by considering the basis for the claim that FDIC resolution should provide the template for the new resolution regime. To do this, we will need to separate wheat from chaff in the administration's appeal to the FDIC model by very briefly exploring the basic contours of the FDIC's historical role and its current powers.

In the oral version of the congressional testimony quoted earlier, Michael Barr characterized the FDIC as having seamlessly handled commercial bank failures for more than 75 years, since its creation in the 1930s. The first thing to note is that this statement is more than a little misleading. For nearly 50 years, from its inception to the 1980s, the FDIC had very little resolution business. Banks very rarely failed during this period, thanks to deposit insurance (which made consumers as comfortable banking with small banks as large ones), the postwar economic boom, and the stable demand for traditional banking services. This period tells us very little about the FDIC's prowess with bank resolution.

The first real test came with the savings and loan (S&L) and banking crisis of the 1980s. As a result of a variety of factors—including deregulation of interest rates on deposits, authorization for S&Ls to buy junk bonds, and collapse of the real estate market in Texas— numerous S&Ls and banks failed over the course of the decade. For those of us who lived through it, the S&L crisis was the biggest financial catastrophe in many years. The debacle ultimately cost taxpayers an estimated $124 billion to clean up. There was near-universal agreement that regulators' failure to close the S&Ls and banks in a timely fashion greatly increased the overall cost.[3]

While regulators' handling of the S&L and bank failures was a disaster, the FDIC does not deserve much of the blame. To start, the FDIC had little to do with the handling of S&L failures; that was the job of the Resolution Trust Corporation. And even with bank resolution, which was its responsibility, the FDIC wasn't the one that decided when it was time to step in. The bank's primary regulator made this decision (as did an S&L's primary regulator in the S&L context). Only after the primary regulator gave the okay could the FDIC sell the bank's assets, restructure it, or shut it down. This feature of the resolution process was widely viewed as its fatal flaw. A regulator who is responsible for a bank's safety and soundness, the reasoning went, will naturally drag his feet in the hope that any bank failure will occur on someone else's watch.

To remedy this and other regulatory flaws, Congress radically restructured banking and S&L regulation, particularly with respect to the resolution process, through the enactment of two laws—the Financial Institutions Reform, Recovery, and Enforcement Act of 1989 (FIRREA) and the FDIC Improvement Act (FDICIA) of 1991. Together, these laws sharply expanded the FDIC's powers. Not only was the FDIC given responsibility for S&L as well as bank resolution, but it also was given the power to close a bank or exercise its other insolvency powers if the bank's primary regulator failed to step in.[4]

Congress didn't simply leave things to the FDIC, however. Congress also enacted (as part of FDICIA) a new set of rules—known as prompt corrective action—that require regulators to take a series of actions as a bank's financial condition deteriorates. The fine details of the prompt corrective action rules need not concern us here, but it may be worth noting that they are keyed to five levels of bank capital, ranging from well-capitalized (Zone 1) to insolvency or nearly so (Zone 5). Starting with Zone 3, FDICIA imposes explicit and increasingly severe sanctions, beginning with a requirement that the bank submit a plan for restoring its capital to appropriate levels. If a bank's net worth falls to 2 percent—that is, its assets are worth 2 percent more than its obligations—or less, regulators are required to step in, take over, and resolve the financial distress.

These rules were intended to ensure that banks would be closed promptly and that their failure would never again impose a serious cost on taxpayers. Because of deposit insurance, the government (and thus taxpayers) is on the hook if a failed bank does not have enough assets to pay its depositors in full. But if banks are closed at or before they become insolvent, the FDIC shouldn't need to tap its deposit insurance fund to pay depositors. This has been especially true since 1993, when deposits were given priority in bank insolvency proceedings.

When advocates of the new Dodd-Frank resolution rules extolled the FDIC, it was this post-1991 framework they really had in mind— the framework that gives the FDIC more authority, and prods regulators with a set of explicit rules as to when and how they should intervene.

At this point, I should briefly describe how the resolution framework is triggered under the new legislation. (For now, I'll be brief. We'll have plenty of space for a more complete overview in Chapter 8.) The rules are designed for the kinds of systemically important institutions we discussed in Chapter 5, although they are not limited to firms that automatically qualify (that is, bank holding companies with $50 billion in assets) or that have been formally designated as systemically important. The decision whether to put a financial company into the resolution regime is governed by a process that has become known as "three keys turning." The three keys are the secretary of the Treasury, the Federal Reserve Board, and the FDIC board. (For investment banks, the third key is the Securities and Exchange Commission [SEC], and for insurance companies it is the director of the new Federal Insurance Office.) If the secretary of the Treasury concludes that the company is "in default or in danger of default," two-thirds of the Federal Reserve Board and two-thirds of the FDIC board have recommended resolution, and the Treasury secretary has also consulted with the President, the secretary can initiate the new resolution process. At this point, the secretary appoints the FDIC as receiver, and the resolution is under way.[5]

You will immediately note, as I did when I began wondering if the FDIC analogy was too good to be true, that the FDIC's role in the process looks rather different in the new resolution regime than with ordinary bank failures. Indeed, the new resolution process begins in an altogether different way. Rather than a series of strict rules dictating when and how they must respond to a company's financial distress, regulators are given substantial discretion whether or when to intervene. And unlike with ordinary bank failures, the FDIC cannot intervene by itself. Nor can anyone else. Under "three keys," there are three decision makers (actually four, if we count the consultation with the President).

If you have followed the discussion thus far especially closely, you may have noticed an irony in the claim that the new resolution regime simply expands the FDIC approach to systemically important institutions. The process for putting a company into resolution doesn't look very much like current FDIC resolution. It looks a lot more like the old, pre-1991 bank insolvency regime—with an ad hoc decision when to intervene and the FDIC initially in a secondary role—than like the current approch.

I should be clear about the point here. I am simply showing how quickly the FDIC analogy breaks down: from the very beginning, with the initial issue of when and how regulators should intervene. I am *not* arguing that the FDIC should have as much control over the decision when to take over a struggling financial giant as it does with ordinary banks. That would make sense only if the FDIC-style resolution will work as well for the largest financial institutions as it does with small and medium-sized banks.

Unfortunately, it won't.

How (and How Well) Does FDIC Resolution Work?

To this point, we have limited our attention to the initial decision whether and when to trigger an insolvency regime. We turn now to the heart of the resolution process. As we consider how current FDIC resolution works, it will quickly become apparent just how much gets lost in translation if we extend the approach to the largest financial institutions, as Dodd-Frank did (though with adjustments, as we explore in Chapter 8).

Unlike bankruptcy, which relies on negotiations between the debtor's managers and its creditors and other stakeholders, with clear rules and opportunities for judicial review throughout the process, commercial bank resolution is a secret, opaque, highly discretionary administrative process centralized in the FDIC. Ordinarily, the FDIC negotiates with one or more healthy banks, and arranges for one to acquire either the troubled bank's deposits (an "insured deposit transfer," which the FDIC uses 34 percent of the time) or the deposits together with some or all of the troubled bank's assets and other liabilities (a "purchase and assumption," used for 54 percent of bank failures). To minimize disruption to depositors' access to their funds and to the payment system generally, regulators typically descend on the troubled bank on a Friday afternoon, and then effect the transfer over the weekend so that the transfer will be complete before the start of business on Monday. The sole constraint on the FDIC's decision about how to resolve the bank's distress is an obligation—another legacy of FDICIA—to select the resolution mechanism that will impose the least cost on the deposit insurance fund.[6]

In arranging the resolution, the FDIC has unfettered control over the treatment of the troubled bank's creditors. Depositors, and the deposit insurance fund, come first for the FDIC, a priority that Congress enshrined in law in 1993 by codifying depositor preference. Deposits are invariably a bank's largest liabilities, dwarfing its other obligations. More than 96 percent of the liabilities of banks with less than $100 million in assets that failed between 1995 and 2009 were deposits. For banks with between $100 million and $500 million in assets the percentage was 92.85 percent; it was roughly 88 percent for banks up to $5 billion, and 70.39 percent for the five megabanks that exceeded $5 billion in assets. Because such a large percentage of a bank's obligations are its deposits, and because depositors get paid before other creditors, most failures do not result in payments to any creditors other than secured creditors and the bank's depositors. But occasionally there is a prospect that other creditors will receive a payout, and in these cases the FDIC determines what that payout will be.[7]

In theory, a disgruntled creditor can challenge either the resolution or the FDIC's treatment of its particular claim. But such a challenge is fraught with obstacles. Because the FDIC acts secretly, creditors cannot question an FDIC action in advance. Any challenge must thus come after the fact. Moreover, the banking laws constrain the grounds for recovery in important respects—limiting it to damages, for instance, and to the difference between the claimant's payout and its likely treatment in a liquidation—and the FDIC's determinations are given de facto deference. In the words of one former FDIC official in an e-mail to my co-author on another project, "there are few cases and changes in the outcome are rare."[8]

While the special FDIC resolution regime for commercial banks is defensible and probably deserves continuing, it is closely tied to the distinctive profile of deposit-taking banks. In any other context, the secretive, ad hoc nature of FDIC resolution would be deeply problematic. But banks have several qualities that make them special. Their financial distress needs to be resolved immediately, because of banks' importance to the nation's payment system and so that consumers need not worry about losing access to their deposits even temporarily. The quick, secretive FDIC process makes this possible.

In addition, because deposits make up such a large percentage of a bank's liabilities, and because the FDIC is responsible for making sure that depositors are paid, it makes sense to let the FDIC decide what to do with the bank's assets. The FDIC and the deposit insurance fund are, in a sense, the only creditors with a real interest in the outcome. Even if the FDIC does not handle the resolution effectively, the harm to the bank's other creditors (or the windfall, in the event the FDIC decides to protect them) is quite limited in most cases.

This, then, is the basic process that was used as the foundation for the new resolution regime. The cases that proponents of Dodd-Frank had in mind when they extolled FDIC resolution were the small and medium-sized bank closings that make up the bulk of the FDIC's work. Between 1995 and 2009, for instance, the FDIC closed 99 banks with assets less than $1 billion (89 of which had assets less than $500 million) and only 20 that exceeded $1 billion in assets.[9]

Even here, with its bread-and-butter bank closings, FDIC resolution has hardly been an unqualified success. Under the mandates of the prompt corrective action rules, the FDIC theoretically should intervene early and should never lose money. But in many cases, things have not worked out this way in practice. In more than two-thirds of the bank closures during the recent crisis, the FDIC's first intervention came when the bank was put in resolution. It never imposed the earlier warning obligations specified by the banking rules. Moreover, the FDIC has lost money in a significant number of these bank closings.[10]

I do not want to denigrate the work done by the FDIC under chairwoman Sheila Bair. Bair has done a tremendous job, and she bravely challenged many of the most problematic features of the early versions of the financial reform legislation. But the suggestion that FDIC resolution is flawless is inaccurate even in ordinary cases. Much more importantly, the FDIC has struggled mightily in nearly all of its larger cases. In these cases, the FDIC has tended to delay intervention, with a strong inclination toward bailouts. The FDIC and thrift regulators waited far too long to close IndyMac, the giant thrift that collapsed in 2008, for instance, and its sale of IndyMac's assets is expected to cost taxpayers roughly $9 billion. It also stumbled in its attempt to resolve Wachovia, brokering a sale to Citigroup that was quickly trumped by Wells Fargo. The sale of Washington Mutual to JPMorgan Chase can perhaps be seen as an exception to the FDIC's difficulties with big banks, but it raises its own concerns, as we will see in a moment.

One obvious reason for the FDIC's poor track record with big banks is that the resolution process is spectacularly ill-suited to large institutions. When the FDIC arranges a purchase and assumption transaction, it ordinarily looks for a larger, healthy bank to acquire the deposits and assets. While this works tolerably well with small and medium-sized commercial banks, the FDIC may find it much more difficult to locate an appropriate buyer for a large bank. There are simply too few possible buyers for the FDIC to consider; and in some cases, there may not be any truly appropriate buyer.

To make matters worse, the FDIC faces a "damned if they do, damned if they don't" predicament. If it finds a buyer, the FDIC will have made a big bank even bigger, thus potentially either creating a bank that is too big to fail or solidifying the too-big-to-fail status of a bank that already fits this description. When the FDIC sold the assets of Washington Mutual to JPMorgan for $1.9 billion, for instance, it made JPMorgan even larger than it already was. No wonder JPMorgan's CEO Jamie Dimon is on so many White House and Washington guest lists.

There is yet another problem with the resolution of a large financial institution like Washington Mutual. A large bank's or S&L's liabilities include far more than deposits alone. In these cases, the FDIC isn't the only real creditor with an interest in the outcome. As a result, the FDIC's dictatorial powers in deciding how to treat particular claims can have a major effect on the bank's creditors. With the Washington Mutual sale, for instance, the FDIC essentially wiped out the subordinated bondholders, arguably giving them much less of a recovery than they would have received in an ordinary bankruptcy proceeding that honored creditors' priorities.[11]

If the FDIC cannot find a buyer, as will often be the case, the "damned if they don't" scenario comes into play. Absent a prospective buyer, the only obvious options are delaying intervention, a bailout, or both. This, in effect, was the government's decision as Citigroup struggled during the financial crisis. Because no one could realistically buy Citigroup, the government propped the giant bank up.

In short, both the unique qualities of commercial banks and the awkward fit between the FDIC's standard resolution techniques and the realities of large banks suggest that the FDIC model—however praiseworthy it may be for smaller banks—cannot comfortably scale up to handle the financial distress of large financial institutions with the requisite transparency and certainty. The new resolution regime thus extends FDIC oversight to precisely the kinds of financial institutions the FDIC has been least effective in handling. The laudable aspects of the FDIC's track record are a tribute to its handling of small and medium-sized bank failures, not the large ones.

Moving Beyond the FDIC Analogy

I have come down hard on the FDIC analogy in this chapter because it played such an insidious role in the debate over the new resolution rules. Like the serpent's appeal to Adam and Eve in the Garden of Eden, it had a seeming logic that derived from the partial truths underlying it. The FDIC has done a reasonably good job of handling bank failures over the past 20 years, as proponents of FDIC-style resolution suggested. But the FDIC does not have the same authority to invoke the new resolution procedures that it has with ordinary banks, and the new provisions extend FDIC-style resolution to precisely the kinds of cases where it is least effective.

Critics of my analysis will no doubt have an important objection at this point. While conceding that the new resolution rules are based on the FDIC's powers for dealing with insolvent banks, they will point out that the Dodd–Frank Act also incorporates many features that are not found in bank insolvency law. Indeed, the drafters of Dodd-Frank borrowed numerous provisions from bankruptcy law, precisely to make the new regime function more like the bankruptcy cases that are my own preferred strategy for handling troubled nonbank financial institutions. Dodd-Frank's resolution rules move well beyond the FDIC analogy, in other words, and need to be considered on their own terms.

This is a fair point, so the next chapter does just this.

Chapter 8

Bailouts, Bankruptcy, or Better? (Resolution Authority II)

A few years from now, Bank of the World (BOW), an imaginary bank that is (let us suppose) one of America's largest financial institutions, is dangerously unstable. A bank with a storied history, BOW expanded rapidly in the 1980s and 1990s, survived the Panic of 2008, and then gambled big on a real estate recovery and new ventures in China and India. Although BOW's investments in China and India have the makings of a brilliant global strategy, the initial costs have been far higher than expected, in part because of unanticipated problems with an Indian subsidiary BOW acquired. Suddenly, hedge funds are pulling their funds from BOW, the price of credit default swap protection on BOW debt has spiked, and rumors are flying that BOW could implode.

The Treasury secretary calls up Bank of the World's chief executive, who says the continuing worldwide slump has made things difficult for BOW and everyone else, but that earnings and the bank's liquidity are fine and the rumors are overblown. Not especially reassured, the Treasury secretary worries that other banks could be vulnerable if BOW were to collapse. He hangs up and calls the chairman of the Federal Reserve, who asks: "What should we do?"

This is the scenario for which the new resolution regime was designed.

Basic Framework

Here, in summary form, are some of the key features we will be considering:

- Triggering the resolution rules:
  - "Three keys turn": Treasury, Federal Reserve, Federal Deposit Insurance Corporation (FDIC).
  - Consultation with President.
- Covered companies: any financial institution.
- Limited judicial review.
- FDIC takes over:
  - Managers replaced if responsible.
  - Shareholders and creditors take losses.
  - Company must be liquidated.

A few basic details will suffice for an initial introduction to the framework. As we saw in Chapter 7, resolution under Dodd-Frank begins when the "three keys turn"—Treasury proposes to take over a systemically important financial company that is in or near default, and the Fed and FDIC concur by a two-thirds vote. The three keys are also expected to consult with the President.

Although the resolution rules clearly are designed for the systemically important institutions we considered in Chapter 5, the framework sweeps much more broadly than this. Regulators can take over any financial institution they wish if they decide that its failure could have a destabilizing effect.

The decision to step in is subject to very little judicial oversight. If the managers of the financial institution do not consent to the government takeover, regulators can initiate the resolution process by filing a petition in federal district court alleging that the company in question is a financial company that is in default or in danger of default. Regulators are not required to make any other showing, and the court can reject the petition only if it is "arbitrary or capricious." The court is given 24 hours to make this determination. Whether this severely truncated review is constitutionally adequate is subject to real question, as we will see.

Once the petition has been filed, the FDIC takes over the company as its receiver, much as the FDIC does with ordinary banks. The FDIC has nearly unfettered discretion to sell the company or any of its parts, either directly or after transferring the assets to a bridge bank. Shareholders are expected to be wiped out, and creditors ordinarily must take losses, except (a major exception) with contracts the FDIC agrees to honor. The objective is to liquidate the company in an orderly fashion, on terms dictated by the FDIC.

To fund the resolution process, the FDIC is entitled to borrow up to 10 percent of the value of the company's assets. With a major financial institution, this will give the FDIC enormous funding capacity— over $200 billion with a company like Citigroup.

Proponents of the new regime claim that it will end taxpayer bailouts and assure an "orderly resolution" of financial distress. Critics insist that it will not end bailouts, and may even make them more likely. Which will it be? And does the new framework improve on ordinary Chapter 11, which it is designed to displace?

To answer these questions, and to chart our path to the heart of the new regime, I will focus on four key objectives that I believe define effective insolvency laws. First, the insolvency framework must be initiated in a timely fashion. Even the most elegant resolution framework won't work if regulators (or the parties themselves, in the case of bankruptcy) wait too long before using it. The second objective is limiting the damaging effect of financial distress on third parties, bystanders to the company's default. In the world of Dodd-Frank, this means limiting systemic risk—the possibility that a major failure will trigger additional failures or paralyze the markets. Third, shareholders and creditors should not be paid in full if the company is insolvent—they should take haircuts, in insolvency lingo. Otherwise, the executives and other shareholders will take too many risks (why not, if it's "heads I win, tails you lose"?), while creditors will be too anxious to lend and will have little reason to monitor the company. Finally, the regime should protect as much of the value of the company's assets as possible—through reorganization, sales of the assets, or by other means. That is, it should facilitate the efficient resolution of financial distress.[1]

I will add texture to each of these factors as we go along. With the second factor, shareholder and creditor haircuts, for instance, transparency and predictability are also important considerations. But focusing on these simple issues will show us what works and does not work in the new resolution regime.

The Trouble with Bailouts

First a few words about those bailouts, to remind us of the alternative that the drafters of Dodd-Frank purport to have ended. I have treated *bailout* as a dirty word throughout the book, and have made no secret of my view that the crisis would have been less severe if Bear Stearns had been allowed to file for bankruptcy. But even I am willing to concede that, in rare circumstances, bailouts can make sense.

The classic candidate for a bailout is a systemically important company that is facing a run on the bank, but is not actually insolvent. In this case, which economists call a liquidity crisis, a quick injection of funds may prevent systemic risk or other collateral damage, and the failure to make shareholders and creditors take a haircut is unproblematic because the financial distress is, in a sense, artificial. It also is not problematic that the insolvency regime is not triggered, and that the company is not restructured. The crisis is like a passing summer storm, whose damage may be prevented by timely intervention.

The classic case is quite rare, however, and regulators have strong incentives to assure us that a bailout is necessary even if it isn't. Default of an important company is messy and can make a regulator's life miserable on many dimensions. Propping the company up for a year or two more with taxpayer funds is often a tempting alternative.

Even the most successful bailouts may have serious downside consequences if the beneficiary is insolvent rather than simply illiquid. The first Chrysler bailout, in 1979 and 1980, was viewed by many as the ultimate bailout success story. The government agreed to guarantee Chrysler's loans, eventually making a profit when the loans were later repaid, and Chrysler's CEO, Lee Iacocca, became a corporate celebrity. But in retrospect we can see that the bailout postponed the more thoroughgoing restructuring the company would have undertaken had it been allowed to file for bankruptcy.

Although Lehman Brothers and American International Group (AIG) were widely acknowledged to have been insolvent in 2008, defenders have suggested that bailouts were necessary to prevent widespread market carnage—that is, systemic consequences of their failures. This conclusion is based in important respects on the Lehman myth that I hope to have put to rest in Chapter 2—the mistaken conventional wisdom that Lehman's bankruptcy triggered the chaos of fall 2008 and showed that bailouts were unfortunate but necessary. Defenders also have often failed to distinguish between ad hoc bailouts and systemwide responses to the crises in the American financial system. In his justly praised book *In Fed We Trust*, David Wessel applauds the welter of extraordinary programs Ben Bernanke and the Federal Reserve put in place in 2008 and 2009 to stabilize the money market, commercial paper, and other markets. These interventions were, on the whole, beneficial, but that doesn't mean that the ad hoc bailouts also were also beneficial.

Even in a crisis, it rarely makes sense to prop up a company that is truly insolvent. To see why, we need to distinguish among three varieties of systemic risk. The first, which economists call an information contagion, is a negative shock that stems from the information that one firm's troubles convey about other firms in the industry. If Bank of the World threatened to collapse, its woes could cause an information contagion in other banks if all of the banks in the industry held significant amounts of the same assets. The discovery that BOW's portfolio of these assets is worth less than everyone thought tells market participants that the other banks' assets are also overvalued, which could lead to a massive devaluation throughout the industry. A second form of systemic crisis—a confidence crisis—is closely related. If Bank of the World's collapse creates uncertainty as to the financial health of other large banks, it may trigger a sudden, marketwide flight by shareholders and creditors of all banks. If the reaction stems from the fact that the banks hold similar assets, it is an information contagion. But if it is based on general uncertainty about the significance of BOW's failure for other banks, it is more aptly described as a confidence crisis.[2]

The final variety of systemic crisis is a counterparty contagion. If other firms are major creditors of Bank of the World, BOW's default and inability to pay may blow a hole in the other companies' own balance sheets. BOW's failure could cause another firm itself to fail, if the firm's exposure to BOW is big enough. If a chain of firms have heavy exposures to one another, BOW's failure could even cause a sequence of failures (domino effect or cascading failures, in the standard argot), including the demise of companies that have no direct connection to BOW.

Of these three kinds of systemic bailout, only a counterparty contagion could plausibly justify the bailout of a particular company. If information contagion or a confidence crisis is severe enough to justify intervention, the government should intervene on a marketwide basis. This, of course, is just what Fed Chair Ben Bernanke did with the extraordinary interventions that Wessel praises, and Congress did with TARP. If the potential crisis is due to counterparty contagion, a targeted bailout might theoretically be possible in order to head off the possibility of multiple failures. But even this is debatable. Even if a failure of Bank of the World could trigger counterparty contagion, it may make more sense to guarantee the debts of the firms that would be affected (as when the Federal Reserve protected the commercial paper market after Lehman defaulted) than to bail out BOW.

Consider what this reasoning tells us about the 2008 crisis. Although systemic crises do not fit neatly into the three boxes I have just described, the Panic of 2008 clearly stemmed far more from an information contagion or a confidence crisis than from a counterparty contagion. At the heart of the problem throughout the crisis was the fact that the largest financial institutions all, though to varying degrees, had major exposure to mortgages and mortgage-related securities. No one knew what they were worth—indeed, we still don't—so turmoil at Bear Stearns or Lehman signaled that there was reason to worry about its peers.

The argument that serious counterparty risk was at stake was based on the concentration of the derivatives industry, with the major players—known before the crisis as the Fourteen Families—heavily connected with one another. If one fell, some have argued, the others could fall. But we now know that Lehman's bankruptcy filing did not lead to the failure of any of the bank's counterparties. To be sure, the Federal Reserve offered a helping hand by guaranteeing some of Lehman's trades shortly after it filed for bankruptcy. But the International Swaps and Derivatives Association—the principal derivatives trade group, and not an organization I typically praise—established a protocol for netting out Lehman's derivatives trades. Within a couple of weeks, the vast majority had been closed out, without any of the counterparties failing.

Americans' deep hostility to the bailouts of Bear Stearns and AIG was thus well-founded. The analysis also suggests that bailing out a troubled firm that would otherwise find itself in insolvency proceedings is rarely justified unless the firm is actually solvent. The only other exception is for a company whose failure would cause a counterparty contagion, which will seldom be the case.

Who Will Invoke Dodd-Frank Resolution, and When?

One of the more surprising attributes of the new legislation—for which the drafters deserve praise—is its effort to make precisely the distinction I have just outlined between systemic responses to a crisis and bailouts of individual firms. When Timothy Geithner and

his colleagues at Treasury outlined their initial financial reform proposal, they did not call for any meaningful constraints on the Federal
Reserve's ability to intervene in a crisis. The Fed's principal legal basis
for extraordinary lending is known as its 13(3) authority, after the
section in the Federal Reserve Act that authorizes the Fed to extend
credit in "unusual and exigent circumstances." This was the Fed's go-
to authority for most of the extraordinary loans and guarantees it made
during the crisis, such as the money market and commercial paper
facilities. In its White Paper, the Treasury proposed only that the Fed
be required to obtain prior written approval from the Treasury before
exercising the extraordinary authority. It is hard to imagine a situation
in which the Treasury—the most political of agencies, whose head
answers directly to the President—would balk at a bailout or other
intervention the Fed wished to make. The Treasury approval requirement was simply window dressing on a proposal that was designed to
institutionalize the bailouts of 2008.[3]

The ostensible theory for the new resolution rules is that they will
displace bailouts as the mechanism for dealing with systemically important financial institutions in distress. Although the Treasury proposal
made no serious effort to achieve this objective, the Dodd-Frank Act
does. In revising the Fed's 13(3) powers, Dodd-Frank retains the prior
approval requirement proposed by the Treasury, but goes substantially
further as well. Not only does the new law state that "emergency lending is for providing liquidity to the financial system and not to aid a
failing financial company," but it amends the authority to allow only
"broad-based" interventions, which are defined to mean interventions that are not aimed at a particular company. (Under the old provision, by contrast, the Fed could lend to any "individual, partnership,
or corporation.") Whether this new restriction will actually prevent
bailouts is subject to question, as we will see; but the revision is clearly
designed to limit bailouts.[4]

The restriction on extraordinary funding of individual companies puts the first of my four insolvency regime factors—timely
initiation—into sharp relief. Will the limitation on Fed funding ensure
that regulators seize control of a floundering, systemically important
financial institution sooner rather than later, without bailing it out?

While no two regulators are alike, any more than two CEOs are, considering the kinds of incentives that Dodd–Frank creates is the best way to predict how each is likely to respond when a bank like Bank of the World is in trouble. The effects of Dodd–Frank could hardly be more dramatic. It does not take a rocket scientist to predict how the major characters, managers especially, will view the new regime. The incentives created by the framework are not encouraging.

Triggering the New Framework

Here, in more detail than our initial discussion, are the key rules for taking a systemically important financial institution down:

- The "three keys": Treasury, two-thirds of Federal Reserve Board, two-thirds of FDIC.
- The initial petition:
  - Filed in federal court in Washington, D.C.
  - Alleges that "covered company" is "in default or is in danger of default," and alternative responses "would have serious adverse effects on financial stability."
- Judicial review: Court can reject only if "arbitrary and capricious"; must decide within 24 hours.
- FDIC generally appointed as receiver:
  - Managers replaced if responsible.
  - Shareholders and creditors take losses.
  - Company must be liquidated.

At the outset, Treasury is the quarterback of the new resolution process. If the Treasury, backed by two-thirds votes of the Federal Reserve and the FDIC, concludes that a financial company is on the verge of default or has defaulted, and that its failure "would have serious adverse effects on financial stability in the United States," it can trigger resolution by filing a petition in federal court in Washington, D.C. Judicial review is extremely limited. So long as it was not "arbitrary and capricious" for regulators to determine that the company is a "financial company" and was in danger of default, the court must sign off on the petition. If Treasury persuades the company to accept the petition, it can avoid review altogether.[5]

While it would be natural to assume that the companies subject to this process are the same ones that we considered in Chapter 5—bank holding companies with more than $50 billion in assets, and nonbanks designated as systemically important—there is no explicit connection. Any financial company—that is, a company that derives at least 85 percent of its earnings from financial activities—can be labeled as a "covered company" and thrown into resolution if the regulators believe that its default would cause financial instability. Surely the two sets of companies will overlap significantly, but regulators' failure to have designated a company as systemically important for the purposes of the new capital requirements and other regulation discussed in Chapter 5 does not preclude them from stepping in under their resolution authority.[6]

If the petition is approved, the FDIC is appointed receiver (other than with investment banks, where the SEC is receiver, and insurance companies, whose receiver is the new federal insurance regulator), and is given extensive authority to borrow money and to take over the company's operations during the receivership. Lest resolution have the appearance of a pleasant landing, the FDIC is instructed to kick out any of the company's managers who are "responsible" for the financial distress, to wipe out shareholders' interests, and to pay creditors whose claims are not assumed (a vital qualification, as we will see later). Unlike either ordinary bank resolution, which permits the FDIC to reorganize a bank through a conservatorship, or bankruptcy, Dodd-Frank resolution provides only for liquidation. Although it may be possible for the FDIC to circumvent this through the creation of a "bridge financial company," the framework is designed with liquidation in mind. A late amendment proposed by Senator Barbara Boxer added an exclamation point, stating that any company in resolution must be liquidated.[7]

It would be hard to overstate how radical these powers are. Bank regulators are likely to postpone resolution if they can, and this problem will be the focus of much of my discussion that follows. But suppose the Treasury secretary in the next crisis decides to take a more aggressive stand—to invoke the resolution rules preemptively and take over Bank of the World? There is very little BOW can do to prevent the preemptive strike, once the Fed and FDIC approve. BOW's only grounds for challenging the petition are that it is not a "financial company" or that it is not "in default or in danger of default." It will be nearly impossible to challenge either—BOW obviously is a financial company and "in danger of default" is broad enough that that will almost certainly be satisfied in any case in which the Treasury secretary is anxious to intervene. BOW is not entitled to challenge any of the other prerequisites for invoking the resolution rules. It cannot object that its default really wouldn't cause financial instability or that a private-sector alternative is available.[8]

The deck is stacked against BOW in other ways as well. The court decision is made within 24 hours, and it is conducted in secret.[9] Moreover, once the court makes its decision, the resolution cannot be put on hold if BOW wishes to pursue an appeal to a higher court. The prospect of stopping even the most outrageous invocation of the new rules is close to nil. Once the company is in resolution, the FDIC has total control.

If your reaction is that this can't possibly be constitutional, you may well be right. There is a very good chance that the resolution rules, with their severe limits on the scope and opportunity to challenge the takeover, violate the due process clause of the Constitution. Due process requires notice and an opportunity to be heard. While the Supreme Court allows Congress to limit due process in some respects, the restrictions on challenge to the resolution rules are so severe as to raise serious Constitutional doubts.[10]

Rather than intervening at the first whiff of trouble and taking advantage of their massive new powers, regulators are more likely to delay their intervention. After all, taking over would mean selling or dismembering a complicated financial institution. Even a Treasury secretary who is less of a bailout enthusiast than Timothy Geithner will want to put off the day of reckoning, and it seems unlikely that the Fed or FDIC will be more anxious to invoke the regime.

Under these circumstances, what are the regulators' options? Although the Fed no longer has carte blanche to make extraordinary loans, there are several ways it could step in, particularly in a crisis. Dodd-Frank authorizes the Fed to guarantee the debt of banking institutions, which would give it considerable power to buttress a bank's stability. While the Fed is now prohibited from making single-company loans, it may be able to circumvent this restriction by establishing a broad-based program that just so happens to benefit a systemically important firm that is stumbling. The program could include restrictions that exclude nearly every firm other than the troubled institution, for instance, or the Fed could simply bail out the industry more broadly. As the Panic of 2008 revealed, regulatory creativity is at its height when regulators are cobbling together a bailout.

Alternatively, using the leverage the Dodd-Frank Act gives them, regulators can force the peer institutions of a troubled bank to pitch in for a bailout. Several of the bailouts of recent decades were privately funded, including the bailout of Long-Term Capital Management in 1998 and a rescue package put together for Korea during roughly the same period. In the past, regulators have been forced to rely on moral suasion, and they couldn't be certain everyone would go along. But, as we saw in Chapter 5, Dodd-Frank has provided the government with new levers to use in its partnership with the largest banks. While a privately-funded bailout does not directly implicate taxpayer funds, it has many of the same pernicious effects.

Even if regulators wanted to intervene in a timely fashion, the complexity of the nation's largest financial institutions is sufficiently great that they are not likely to know until late in a company's decline that the time has come. If regulators are making the decision when to invoke Dodd-Frank resolution, it will come either too late or even (if the company is bailed out) never.

The people who are likely to have the best information about the company's condition are, of course, its managers. With ordinary companies, Chapter 11 is well designed to encourage the managers to take matters into their own hands when a company is in trouble. In Chapter 11, the managers continue to run the business after it files for bankruptcy, and they are the only ones who can propose a reorganization plan for the first six months of the case, and often longer.[11] Although shareholders do not receive anything in many cases, they sometimes end up with something, either because the company does well during the bankruptcy or because shareholders succeed in negotiating at least a limited payment for themselves. These attributes of Chapter 11 encourage managers to file for bankruptcy in a timely fashion.

Because the Dodd-Frank resolution regime dispenses with these carrots, the managers of a company like Bank of the World have no reason to point the company toward resolution. Indeed, much as with Lehman and AIG, the managers have every reason to make a potential resolution look as messy as possible in the hope of securing a bailout or persuading regulators to delay intervention.

Dodd-Frank does have one important provision that could limit managers' ability to ensure that resolution would mean chaos. Systemically important companies are now required to file a so-called living will—a report that details how the company could be closed down in orderly fashion if it were to descend into financial distress. If regulators demand detailed and plausible resolution plans, the living wills could avert some of the disruption of a default. Regulators might even presumptively commit to following the course of action outlined in the living will in the event they later invoked the resolution rules. But the living will requirement applies only to companies that have been formally designated as systemically important. And managers are unlikely to devise serious and realistic plans unless regulators are unusually vigilant in enforcing the new obligation.[12]

An interesting question is whether the managers of a company like Bank of the World will file for bankruptcy as an alternative to resolution. Bankruptcy is not a great career move for the managers of a financial institution, but it does have the advantages I mentioned earlier: The managers continue to run the business, and they are the only ones who can propose a reorganization plan—or other action, such as a sale of the company's assets—for a period of time.

Compared to Dodd-Frank resolution, bankruptcy doesn't look so bad, but it has several important limitations from the managers' perspective. The first is that, if the managers file for bankruptcy, Dodd-Frank gives bank regulators the power to pull the case out and put it in resolution. Resolution trumps bankruptcy, so a Chapter 11 filing could simply prove to be a temporary reprieve, before regulators take over. Second, although managers do retain their jobs at first, they are likely to be forced to step down before the case reaches its conclusion. Finally, derivatives and other financial contracts are not subject to core bankruptcy provisions such as the automatic stay, which limits the managers' ability to arrange a sale or other disposition of the company's assets. (I will revisit the problematic effect of these rules in Chapter 9 when proposing ways to limit some of Dodd-Frank's flaws.)

Given these limitations, Chapter 11 is a risky option from a manager's perspective—better, but only marginally so, than Dodd-Frank's harsh medicine. From their perspective, sticking with the business and forgoing any meaningful disaster planning is likely to be the best bet.

Because neither of the principal parties—regulators or managers—will be anxious for Dodd-Frank to be invoked, timely initiation is unlikely.

Controlling Systemic Risk

The case for a governmental resolution regime rested on two claims: the FDIC analogy we dissected in Chapter 7, and the contention that only administrative resolution can prevent systemic crises. Controlling systemic risk, the second objective of an effective insolvency regime, is indeed the one thing Dodd-Frank may do tolerably well. But it will do so by smuggling bailouts into the resolution regime.

Two sets of rules lie at the heart of Dodd-Frank's response to systemic risk, both borrowed from FDIC resolution of ordinary banks. The first is a special set of rules for derivatives and other financial instruments—known as qualified financial contracts (QFCs) in the banking world. The second is broad discretion for the FDIC to fund almost anything it wants. Whatever bailout authority was siphoned off from the Fed outside of resolution has reappeared in the hands of the FDIC in the new regime.

Here is a summary of the key rules:

- Rules for QFCs (derivatives):
  - Ipso facto clauses: unenforceable for one business day.
  - Master agreement: treated as single contract.
  - All or nothing: FDIC must assume all or none with each party.

- FDIC's power of the purse:
  - Broad funding discretion: can buy or guarantee assets.
  - Huge borrowing capacity: up to 10 percent of value of preresolution assets; 90 percent postresolution.
  - FDIC borrowing entitled to priority.
  - Source of funds: any remaining obligations paid for by assessments on large financial institutions.

In the standard swap contract, bankruptcy or insolvency proceedings are an event of default, entitling the other party to cancel the contract and sell any collateral. In bankruptcy, these provisions—known as ipso facto clauses—are fully enforceable. If a systemically important institution like Bank of the World—or AIG in 2008—filed for bankruptcy, all of these counterparties theoretically could cancel their contracts at the same time. If everyone sold their collateral at once, it could drive down asset prices and exacerbate an existing crisis. In 2008, for instance, sales of the mortgage-related securities that AIG had posted as collateral could have sent mortgage values spiraling down even more.

Dodd-Frank resolution addresses this risk by putting the counterparties' right to cancel their contracts on hold for a brief period of time. The FDIC has until 5 P.M. the next business day to decide how to handle these financial contracts. Although the delay is often described as one day, regulators could stretch it to nearly four days if they cleverly timed the beginning of the resolution. If the resolution began early on a Friday morning, the enforcement ban would last until 5 P.M. on Monday, since Monday is the next business day.[13]

During this time (and after, if the other party doesn't cancel the contract), the FDIC has the decision whether to repudiate the contracts or promise to pay them in full. In deference to the derivatives industry, Dodd-Frank imposes two related constraints on the FDIC's options at this point. The first is that, if the troubled bank has a master agreement covering a variety of different transactions with the same counterparty—which is standard practice with derivatives—the FDIC must give the same treatment to all of the contracts, either keeping them or repudiating them. Second, the same principle applies more generally to all of a debtor's swaps with a particular party. The FDIC's choice is all or nothing. It must repudiate all of the contracts or none of them.[14]

Although current FDIC chair Sheila Bair is a tough-minded regulator and not so enamored of bailouts as Treasury Secretary Geithner is, she surely would respond in similar fashion if a large institution like Bank of the World were put in resolution. Faced with an all-or-nothing decision, she or any other FDIC chair would guarantee all of the derivatives with all of BOW's major counterparties, rather than risk systemic problems. If most of the contracts were subject to clearinghouse arrangements, the pressure to honor all the contracts might be reduced somewhat, but the FDIC will still worry about the effect of repudiation on the clearinghouses, and the risk that sales of the accompanying collateral by the clearinghouses could have a systemic effect.

The fact that the FDIC chair will not be making the repudiation decision in isolation will add further pressure to rescue the derivatives contracts. Both the Fed and the Treasury must also approve the decision to put the company in resolution, which will give each the opportunity to insist that the derivatives need to be protected.

The special derivatives rules create a strong temptation to rescue these contracts, as we have just seen, and Dodd-Frank's financing rules provide both funding and authority to take other rescue actions as well. Dodd-Frank invites the FDIC to purchase or guarantee the company's assets, to assume or guarantee its debts, or to intervene in almost any way it wishes. To finance these interventions, Dodd-Frank authorizes the FDIC to harness the borrowing power of the U.S. Treasury, issuing Treasury obligations up to 10 percent of the value of the company's pre-resolution consolidated assets during the first 30 days of the case, and up to 90 percent of the value in resolution thereafter.[15] To visualize how much funding this is, consider that Lehman Brothers reported $639 billion in assets when it filed for bankruptcy. Under the new Dodd-Frank resolution, the FDIC would have had $63.9 billion at its disposal during the first 30 days of the case. With Citigroup or Bank of America, the FDIC would have more than $200 billion.

If there is a virtue to this massive honey pot, it is the FDIC's flexibility to prevent systemic crises. Protecting the creditors of a troubled company is one response to systemic risk, although industry-wide responses will more often be effective, as we have seen. And the vice of the FDIC's sweeping authority is that it invites interventions that are essentially bailouts.

Dodd-Frank does try to limit *taxpayers'* responsibility for the costs of the FDIC's funding decisions. The FDIC obligations—which will initially be funded as debt issued by the Treasury—are given priority status in the resolution through provisions that instruct the FDIC to pay itself before paying ordinary creditors. For any costs that aren't covered in the resolution proceeding itself, Dodd-Frank provides for payment from an Orderly Liquidation Fund, to be paid for through assessments imposed on other systemically important institutions after the resolution.

These provisions are the basis for Dodd-Frank enthusiasts' claims that the legislation has ended taxpayer-funded bailouts, culminating with a triumphant "never again" from President Obama when he signed the legislation. That isn't the case, since we still may see bailouts outside of the resolution regime. But even in the absence of a preresolution bailout, FDIC intervention may have many of the same damaging effects as a bailout—and indeed, will be a bailout, as I explain in the next section. It just won't be a taxpayer-funded bailout.

Third Objective: Haircuts

The third objective of an effective insolvency regime is to ensure that the shareholders and creditors of an insolvent company suffer losses roughly consistent with the priority of their interest and the value of the floundering company. Suppose, for instance, that the value of the company's assets is $100, and that it owes $80 to Senior Creditor, whose claim is collateralized by all of the assets; it owes $50 to Junior Creditor, a general creditor; and there is one Shareholder, who also is the company's manager. If this company defaults, we would expect the insolvency regime to ensure that Senior Creditor is paid in full,

Junior receives most or all of the $20 that remains (but loses $30), and Shareholder's interests are wiped out. In its strict form, this general principle is known as the absolute priority rule. We may have good reason to depart from it in some respects. Giving Shareholder a small payment may make Shareholder more willing to put the company into an insolvency proceeding sooner rather than later, for instance. But an effective insolvency regime should generally stick with absolute priority.

If the government steps in and bails out Junior Creditor or Shareholder, or both, by contrast, promising to pay them in full, the bailout introduces serious distortions. The managers and shareholders of companies similar to this one may adopt risky strategies—such as the extraordinary leverage taken on by investment banks like Bear Stearns and Lehman—on the assumption that the rewards of success will be great if the gamble succeeds, while they won't be punished if it fails. This phenomenon—risk taking by those who are protected against risk—is the familiar problem known as moral hazard. Similarly, junior creditors will be more willing lend to companies like this one and may not spend much time monitoring its performance, if they expect the government to ensure they will be paid in full. Peter Wallison has dubbed the credit market distortions this creates the "Fannie Mae effect," in reference to the artificially low borrowing costs Fannie Mae and Freddie Mac enjoyed due to the government's implicit guarantee of their debt before they were formally nationalized in 2008.

During the 2008 crisis, the three regulatory musketeers—Paulson, Geithner, and Bernanke—went to great lengths to prevent shareholder moral hazard. Paulson was so anxious to make sure that managers and shareholders were punished that he pressured JPMorgan to *lower* the price it offered for Bear Stearns from $4 to $2 per share (JPMorgan ended up paying $10 per share).[16] The triumvirate forced AIG's chief executive to step down, and drastically diluted its shareholders' interests, for the same reason.

Although the regulators initially claimed that their interventions weren't bailouts, in each case the government fully protected the company's creditors. The expectation that creditors would be bailed out, and the distortions this creates (credit subsidies for favored firms and creditor moral hazard), explains why prices for the bonds of the biggest financial institutions stayed so high throughout the crisis, and the prices for credit default swaps on Lehman did not anticipate its default. The bailouts of 2008 were creditor bailouts.

The Dodd-Frank resolution regime (once again departing from the original Treasury proposal) announces a policy of forcing shareholders and creditors to take haircuts in resolution, and of throwing the managers out. According to a provision labeled "mandatory terms," the FDIC shall:

> ensure that the shareholders of a covered financial company do not receive payment until all of the claims and the Fund are fully paid; . . . ensure that unsecured creditors bear losses in accordance with the priority of claim provisions . . . ; [and] ensure that management responsible for the failed condition of the covered financial company is removed.[17]

In addition to this "mandatory" priority structure, the new regime includes a cluster of provisions, most borrowed from bankruptcy law, that have related concerns in mind. The FDIC is authorized to retrieve payments made to a creditor during the 90 days before the start of resolution, and to invalidate sales or other transfers of the company's property if the company received less than the property was worth. (These are known as preference and fraudulent conveyance powers.) In addition, if any creditor is given more than the claim it would receive in a bankruptcy liquidation, the creditor is required to give the difference back to the FDIC. Each of these rules is designed to ensure that similarly situated creditors are treated the same, and to police situations that have the effect of giving priority treatment to some creditors and not others.[18]

For anyone who is familiar with ordinary bank resolution, these provisions will come as a refreshing surprise. When it closes an ordinary bank, the FDIC has broad discretion in determining which claims get paid, and to what extent. This means that basic priorities may not be respected. It also means that creditors cannot predict in advance how they will be treated. Dodd-Frank seems to have a much more formal and transparent priority structure.

Unfortunately, the rules will prove irrelevant in practice for many of the financial institution's largest and most important claims. The problem is that these careful priority requirements, with all of their sensible adjustments, can easily be evaded. As with ordinary bank resolution, Dodd-Frank resolution gives the FDIC blanket authority to pay claims in full if it wishes, as we saw in our discussion of systemic risk. As the receiver of a company like Bank of the World, the FDIC will likely pay off all or almost all of the derivatives and other financial claims, and perhaps other claims as well. Although these creditors theoretically must give some of their recovery back if other creditors receive less than they would get in a liquidation, the FDIC can simply give the other creditors a pittance and argue that this is more than a bankruptcy liquidation would have brought. Had there been a bankruptcy, the FDIC might say, the firm's value would have evaporated and creditors would have gotten almost nothing. Using this reasoning, the FDIC can easily bail out the most important creditors while giving little or nothing to other, theoretically comparable claims.

As President Obama once said in another context, the priority rules are just lipstick on a pig.

All Liquidation, All the Time?

We come now to the final objective of an effective insolvency regime: resolving the company's financial distress efficiently, to protect as much value as possible.

In my dissection of the FDIC analogy in the preceding chapter, I pointed out that the standard FDIC strategy for closing an ordinary bank is much dicier for a systemically important financial institution. With the little banks that are its bread and butter, the FDIC secretly lines up a buyer if the bank is failing, closes the bank at the end of the day on Friday, and then completes the sale in time for customers to have access to their deposits and for businesses to have access to their lines of credit on Monday morning. With the largest banks and nonbank financial institutions, by contrast, the number of plausible buyers is far smaller. It will be more difficult, and sometimes impossible, to arrange a sale. Who exactly would buy Citigroup or Bank of America if it were sinking? And because the potential buyers are other large financial institutions, the sales that do occur will make a financial giant even bigger.

The drafters of Dodd-Frank compounded this problem by limiting the FDIC to a single set of resolution options: liquidation. Prior to a late amendment proposed by Senator Boxer, this restriction would not have been obvious to anyone but a banking nerd. It is signaled in Dodd-Frank by the appointment of the FDIC as receiver of the troubled institution, the references to the regime as "receivership," and the absence of any mention of "conservatorship." Conservatorship is the principal—though rare—technique for reorganizing a troubled bank rather than selling it or shutting it down. Thanks to the Boxer amendment, this careful parsing of the resolution regime is no longer necessary. The new law could not put it more clearly: "All financial companies put into receivership under this title shall be liquidated. No taxpayer funds shall be used to prevent the liquidation of any financial company under this title."[19]

It is theoretically possible for clever regulators to restructure a financial company rather than truly liquidating it. As an alternative to arranging an immediate merger or piecemeal liquidation, Dodd-Frank authorizes the FDIC to transfer assets and liabilities to a "bridge financial company." The bridge company is designed to be temporary, but Dodd-Frank allows it to continue for up to three years. By picking and choosing which assets and liabilities to transfer to the bridge company, and subsequently merging it with another firm or selling stock to investors, the FDIC could achieve a de facto reorganization.[20]

This stands in obvious tension with the Boxer amendment's proclamation that the company "shall be liquidated," but this violation of the Boxer amendment's spirit is unlikely to prevent disguised reorganizations. The more important obstacle is the centrality of regulators, rather than the parties themselves. The FDIC is not set up to oversee a major financial institution for long enough to achieve a genuine reorganization or even a more patient liquidation. After IndyMac failed in 2008, for instance, the FDIC sold its assets much more quickly than many observers thought optimal, because of its reluctance to manage assets for a substantial period of time. "When the FDIC steps in," as one account of its role in the new resolution framework put it, "it assumes control over all assets and operations. The goal is not to save the company. On the contrary, it's to liquidate it in an orderly way that maximizes its value."[21]

This bias toward liquidation marks a radical change in American insolvency regulation. The distinctively American response to the financial distress of large corporations emerged in the late nineteenth century during periodic crises in the railroad industry. At the behest of the Wall Street banks that financed the railroads and the banks' lawyers, American courts devised a procedure known as the equity receivership—which was the ancestor of and inspiration for current Chapter 11. The premise, then as now, was that reorganization is often the most efficient method of resolving financial distress, especially with the largest companies—that reorganization can preserve value that would otherwise be lost.[22]

Some may object here that financial institutions are different from other large corporations in this regard. The value of a commercial bank, the reasoning goes, disappears in a cloud of smoke as soon as it defaults. While this may be true of the commercial bank entity itself, it does not accurately describe bank holding companies or other financial institution holding companies—each of whose insolvencies were handled only in bankruptcy prior to the Dodd-Frank Act. For some of these a restructuring may be far superior to a receivership, particularly if there are no or few potential buyers for the company's assets. Restructuring a troubled financial institution could also promote competition in the financial services industry, by preserving a competitor rather than shrinking the industry through the liquidation of one of a limited number of giant companies.

Dodd-Frank doesn't take these options off the table altogether, but it makes them far less likely. This increases the potential for value to be squandered in connection with a Dodd-Frank resolution—a risk that is particularly serious given the limitations of FDIC-style resolution with the largest financial institutions.

■ ■ ■

By my reckoning in this chapter, Dodd-Frank resolution is ill-equipped to handle three of the four objectives of an insolvency regime. The decision when to put a company in resolution will be made by regulators, rather than managers and market participants. This makes timely intervention unlikely; it and the prospect of immediate ouster will discourage the managers of a floundering financial giant from making any preparations for an orderly resolution. Because the FDIC can pay any creditors it wishes, there is no assurance that any given class of creditors—such as those holding derivatives—will be forced to take losses. And Dodd-Frank discourages and purports to forbid reorganization, even if that may be the best resolution option.

The only objective that Dodd-Frank handles tolerably well is limiting the danger of systemic risk. The same FDIC powers that make the promise of creditor haircuts illusory and undermine the priority scheme will enable the FDIC to respond to the threat of systemic risk by protecting vulnerable parties. The FDIC can promise to make good on the company's derivatives, for instance, if it concludes that mass repudiation could ignite a systemic crisis.

Assessing an insolvency regime is not simply a matter of adding up the grades on the various attributes of the framework, and tallying up the score, of course. Perhaps the best defense of the Dodd-Frank regime comes by analogy to Winston Churchill's famous defense of democracy: Dodd-Frank is the worst possible strategy for handling the financial distress of systemically important financial institutions—except, that is, for all the others.

But the Churchill dictum doesn't hold true here. The only thing that the Dodd-Frank resolution rules do at all well—responding to systemic risk—will soon be less crucial for most financial institutions, thanks to other, more effective parts of the Dodd-Frank Act. If most of the company's derivatives are backstopped by a clearinghouse, for instance, it will be much less important that the FDIC step in and make sure they all are honored.

Some have defended the resolution rules by emphasizing that they displace the normal, rule-of-law-oriented bankruptcy process for only a small group of companies, the very largest financial institutions. The hole may be deep, the argument goes, but it is narrow. But this reasoning is highly misleading. The "small" number of institutions covered by the new rules isn't so small. It already consists of the 36 bank holding companies with more than $50 billion in assets, and it will expand to include the nonbank financial institutions the Financial Stability Oversight Council deems systemically important, plus any other financial companies whose financial distress seems to regulators to jeopardize the nation's financial stability. Not only is this a sizable group, but each of its members dwarfs all but a handful of ordinary businesses in size. Their significance far outstrips their number.

These financial giants are now subject to an ad hoc, unpredictable insolvency process. No one knows for sure who is subject to it, since regulators can decide at the last minute that a financial company is in danger of default and that its default would pose a risk to financial stability. If regulators decide to take over, it will be essentially impossible for the company to resist, since the company is given almost no time and no basis for resisting—in violation of the ordinary right to due process. Once resolution is under way, regulators can pick and choose which claims to pay and which not to pay. The rule of law takes a backseat as soon as regulators begin thinking about intervening.

Thus, the bad news: The Dodd-Frank resolution is a mess. The good news is that it can be salvaged. I believe that the most serious problems can be fixed through simple adjustments to the ordinary bankruptcy laws to encourage troubled companies to initiate voluntary bankruptcy proceedings in the event of a crisis. Those adjustments are the subject of the next chapter, which shifts from description and diagnosis to possible cures.

Part III

THE FUTURE

Chapter 9

Essential Fixes and the New Financial Order

The 2,319 pages of the Dodd-Frank Act have two overriding themes: partnership between the government and an oligarchy of the largest financial institutions, and ad hoc intervention in a crisis. The legislation takes the dominance of a handful of financial institutions, including commercial banks, investment banks, and possibly others, as a given, and cements their position as the gatekeepers of American finance. These institutions, in turn, will be expected to serve as channels for political concerns of the government. In a crisis, regulators will bail them out or take them over.

Although some Republican lawmakers called for repeal of Dodd-Frank even before it was officially signed into law, the new legislation is with us to stay. There is no politically plausible scenario under which its key planks will be reversed, however much its opponents hope that shifts in Congress will make this an option in the coming years.

The fact that the new legislation is permanent makes the exercise that we have been pursuing—considering what Dodd-Frank will do and what it means—all the more important. But it is also important to consider whether there are any simple ways that the new regulatory regime could be improved—reforms that could counteract some of its obvious flaws with targeted amendments that might be broadly popular and would not require lawmakers to undo their 2,319 pages of handiwork.

Is it possible that silver bullets like these—small adjustments that could make a big difference—actually exist? I believe that they do. Perhaps I should have called this entire chapter "Bankruptcy to the Rescue" (instead of just the final section), because bankruptcy is where several of the most promising opportunities for reform lie. To show why we need bankruptcy and its rule-of-law virtues more than ever, the chapter begins by describing the attributes of the new partnership between government and the largest banks that most need fixing. The remainder of the chapter is devoted to several bankruptcy reforms that could help to reorient Dodd-Frank.

What Works and What Doesn't

Although it radically departs from the regulatory strategy of the past 75 years—which favored competition and a less concentrated financial services industry—the European-style partnership between the government and the largest financial institutions introduced by the Dodd-Frank Act has strengths as well as weaknesses. If bank regulators monitor the new clearinghouses effectively and if they implement the new bank capital requirements vigorously, the financial system will be much less risky and crisis prone than it was before the financial crisis. These are big ifs, to be sure. Capital requirements, for instance, have often been more effective in concept than in practice, which cautions against the more optimistic expectations of their likely success. But a corporatist partnership between the government and the largest banks does have the advantage of comparative stability. The risk of disruption certainly hasn't disappeared, but it is now lower than it was before Dodd-Frank was enacted.

As we have seen throughout the book, however, the new approach has very pronounced dark sides. The largest financial institutions will be able to borrow money more cheaply than their smaller competitors. The disadvantage for smaller institutions will be especially pronounced in capital-intensive areas like derivatives, which already are highly concentrated. Here and elsewhere, Dodd–Frank will multiply the Fannie Mae effect.

The government-bank partnership also depends heavily on regulator expertise. For the government's partnership with industry to work, the regulators must be capable of keeping one step ahead of industry leaders and the market. In a fully corporatist system, the industry giants may be so dependent on the government that this is not a major problem. But if the large financial institutions have more flexibility, as is much more likely under Dodd–Frank, regulatory competence is a serious issue.

There have been brief periods of time in American history when regulators may have had as much expertise, or nearly so, as the banks and businesses they regulated. At the outset of the New Deal, for instance, many top scholars and market-savvy Wall Street insiders were attracted to Washington. Joseph Kennedy, the somewhat shady businessman and father to the future President, was brought in (with grumbling in some quarters that the fox would be guarding the henhouse) to head the Securities and Exchange Commission (SEC) at its inception. And top scholars like Yale Law School Professor William O. Douglas and his former Columbia colleague Jerome Frank joined the administration in regulatory roles. But these situations have never lasted, even in heavily regulatory eras. The pay differential is too stark, as is the lure of being where the action is.[1]

One risk is simply that regulators will be outmaneuvered by those they are supposed to regulate—which is a familiar concern in the relationship between Wall Street and Washington. But at least as serious is the fact that because the key decisions are made by regulators, private parties have less autonomy, especially in times of crisis, and they will not have adequate incentives to use their superior knowledge and expertise. As we saw in the preceding chapter, this is a particular problem with the new resolution rules. Because resolution is run entirely by regulators, and the managers of a troubled financial institution will likely be ousted, the managers have no reason to prepare for a default or to contribute to the initiation decision. And if regulators do finally intervene, their intervention is not constrained by general rule-of-law principles.

The ideal adjustments would be those that might reduce the dependence of the new regime on regulators, give private parties more of an incentive to bring their superior knowledge to bear, and reinforce traditional rule-of-law values. Not an easy task, but several comparatively simple bankruptcy reforms would help.

Staying Derivatives in Bankruptcy

The first reform would simply remove a set of special protections that derivatives and other financial innovations are given in bankruptcy. These protections are relics of an era—the past 30 years—when the Federal Reserve, Treasury, and derivatives trade groups persuaded Congress that the derivatives markets could regulate themselves and needed to be protected from interference. It became clear during the financial crisis that the special treatment of derivatives is a mistake. As I will explain later, the special treatment interfered with the ability of Bear Stearns, Lehman Brothers, and American International Group (AIG) to slow their downward spiral. This in itself would be reason to reverse the special treatment and to treat derivatives counterparties the same way as other creditors. But there is a far more powerful reason to remove the special treatment as well. Treating derivatives the same way as other contracts would give the managers of troubled financial institutions much greater incentives to make adequate preparation for insolvency proceedings, and to use bankruptcy rather than the Dodd–Frank resolution regime.[2]

The thought of discussing derivatives and bankruptcy at the same time may sound daunting for those who are not aficionados of both. But bear with me. The reasoning is relatively straightforward, and its implications could not be more important.

Nearly every other creditor in bankruptcy is subject to a basic set of core bankruptcy rules. Of particular importance is the automatic stay. The stay is the bankruptcy equivalent of a cease and desist order; it prohibits creditors from grabbing collateral, pursuing legal actions, or pestering the debtor for what they are owed. The stay is designed to give the debtor a breathing space to decide how best to resolve the financial distress. Bankruptcy also prohibits creditors from enforcing provisions in their contracts (known as ipso facto clauses) that allow the creditor to terminate the contract if the debtor files for bankruptcy. Under bankruptcy's preference and fraudulent provisions, creditors are required to give back payments they receive shortly before bankruptcy and property that was transferred to them for less than it was worth.[3]

Derivatives and other financial instruments are protected from all of these rules. If a systemically important financial institution like Bank of the World (BOW) is in precarious financial condition, its derivatives counterparties may demand more collateral for their contracts and its repo lenders may threaten not to renew their loans. Suppose, for instance, that the counterparty on a portfolio of credit default swaps has $20 million of collateral and insists that BOW pony up an additional $80 million in collateral because it is now worried that BOW may default. Most creditors would be required to give the $80 million in new collateral back if BOW filed for bankruptcy shortly after it was posted; collateral grabs on the eve of bankruptcy are treated as impermissible preferences. But the credit default swap creditor is exempt from this requirement. Nor can BOW stop the creditor from terminating the contract and selling the collateral.[4]

These special rules were the fruit of a 30-year campaign, dating back to the enactment of the current bankruptcy laws in 1978, by the Fed, Treasury, and industry trade groups to insulate derivatives from bankruptcy. These groups argued that if derivatives were not completely protected from the automatic stay, a bankruptcy involving a firm with significant derivatives exposure could snarl the financial system. As a representative from the Fed put it in a 1999 submission to Congress:

> [T]he right to terminate or close-out financial market contracts
> is important to the stability of financial market participants . . .
> and reduces the likelihood that a single insolvency will trigger

other insolvencies due to the non-defaulting counterparties' inability to control their market risk. The right to terminate or close-out protects [financial institutions] . . . on an individual basis, and by protecting both the supervised and unsupervised market participants, protects the markets from systemic problems of "domino failures."[5]

If derivatives were protected from bankruptcy, by contrast, the market would clean up its own messes. When an investment bank or other participant in the derivatives industry filed for bankruptcy, advocates argued, the counterparties to its outstanding derivatives contracts could quickly terminate the contracts and—if the contracts were designed as a hedge against risk—enter into replacement contracts.

These optimistic promises proved misplaced during the 2008 crisis. The same regulatory agencies that had extolled the benefits of special treatment—a stance that spanned both Democratic and Republican administrations, and included even Paul Volcker during his stint as Fed chair—feared that the termination of hundreds of thousands of derivatives contracts at the same time if an institution like AIG filed for bankruptcy might itself cause a systemic crisis. If the counterparties to AIG's credit default swaps terminated and sold their collateral, the sales might drive down the value of the assets, many of which were mortgage-related.

Although the concerns were undoubtedly overstated, they highlight a serious cost of the special treatment for derivatives: It takes away the ability of a financial institution to use bankruptcy to put a temporary halt to a run by its derivatives creditors. From AIG's or Lehman's perspective, there was no reason to prepare for bankruptcy and no benefit to using it, since a considerable part of the firm's hemorrhaging wouldn't be arrested by filing for bankruptcy.

The special derivatives rules have damaging effects long before a financial institution finds itself in financial distress as well. One serious problem is that the special treatment makes derivatives and repos an irresistible way to borrow money as compared to traditional loans. Because these creditors can immediately grab and sell any collateral they have if the debtor files for bankruptcy, whereas traditional lenders are subject to the stay and therefore must wait, they will offer more attractive terms than traditional lenders. A 2005 amendment to the bankruptcy laws expanded the class of repos that receive special protection to include repos of risky assets like the mortgage-backed securities held by Bear Stearns and Lehman, which may have magnified the attraction of repo financing. This wouldn't be problematic if there were no significant differences between repos and derivatives, on the one hand, and traditional forms of financing, on the other. But derivatives and repos are much more volatile. They can be quickly withdrawn, immediately sapping a financial institution's liquidity.[6]

The bias toward derivatives and repos is bad enough with ordinary financial institutions; it is radically worse with systemically important ones. An institution like Bank of the World may well be bailed out if it stumbles. At the least, the Federal Deposit Insurance Corporation (FDIC) can be expected to ensure that its derivatives are paid in full in a resolution, as we saw in Chapter 8. This surely is at least one reason that the percentage of financing that Bear Stearns obtained from repos climbed from 7 percent of its liabilities and twice its equity in 1990 to 25 percent and eight times its equity in 2008, as one prominent scholar has shown.[7]

The prospect of protection introduces other problems as well. Derivatives and repo creditors have much less incentive to monitor and to sound the alarm when the institution is in trouble if they are confident they will be bailed out if the company fails. The incentive to monitor will not disappear altogether, of course, and some creditors may even monitor actively. During the financial crisis, repo creditors kept close tabs on Bear Stearns and Lehman. But other creditors, such as derivatives counterparties, were less vigilant. Their disincentive to monitor—recall the tardy response of the credit default swap market to Lehman's problems from Chapter 2—means that some of the most sophisticated players in the marketplace may stay on the sidelines when their expertise is needed most.

Still another problem is that the parties that enter into derivatives with a bank like Bank of the World will not be as careful to limit their exposure to BOW if they anticipate that they will be bailed out. Rather than spreading their derivatives business among a multitude of counterparties, they can feel free to load up on derivatives with BOW. (The new clearinghouses could even exacerbate this tendency, since they create an even stronger sense of protection for derivatives that are subject to clearing.) By lowering the risks of having a large exposure to any given counterparty, the special derivatives rules have thus diminished the incentives for a bank to spread its derivatives business around, and have abetted the dominance of the derivatives industry by a small number of the biggest financial institutions.

A philosopher once pointed out that a small rudder can steer a giant vessel, causing it to change direction. Simple legal reforms rarely have this much power. But reversing the special treatment of derivatives comes close.

If derivatives and other financial instruments were subject to the same core bankruptcy principles as other contracts—such as the stay and the preference rules—the bias toward derivatives-based and repo financing would be significantly reduced. Derivatives creditors would pay much closer attention to a debtor's financial condition, and they would be more careful to limit their exposure to any particular institution, particularly with derivatives that are not backstopped by a clearing organization.

The most dramatic implications, however, would be for the managers of an institution like Bank of the World. Ending the special treatment for derivatives would completely alter their perspective if BOW were to fall into financial distress. The prospect of a stay would make bankruptcy a temporary safe haven, as it is for other companies. The knowledge that they had the option of filing for bankruptcy and obtaining a stay would enable BOW's managers to resist collateral demands that might otherwise dismember the firm as its fortunes deteriorated, as was happening with AIG before it was bailed out. The managers also would have every reason to plan for an orderly bankruptcy, since they would continue to run the business in bankruptcy and could use the breathing space provided by the stay to arrange for an efficient disposition of BOW's assets through a sale, a reorganization, or some combination of the two. The simple expedient of giving managers the benefit of the stay would make bankruptcy a much more viable option for a systemically important firm.

To put the point in slightly different terms, if the special treatment of derivatives were reversed, the Dodd-Frank resolution regime would rarely, if ever, be necessary. The managers of a troubled, systemically important financial institution would take matters into their own hands, preparing for and filing a bankruptcy case on their own if trouble arose. With bankruptcy would come procedural fairness, transparency, and the full complement of rule-of-law values that are undermined by the Dodd-Frank resolution framework.

ISDA and Its Discontent

Not everyone loves the proposal to remove the special treatment that derivatives currently receive in bankruptcy. The principal critic of the proposal has been the principal advocate of special treatment, the International Swaps and Derivatives Association (ISDA), the industry trade and lobbying group. In one of its recent research memos, ISDA dismissed the kinds of arguments I have made in earlier work as "radical suggestions, mostly from academic researchers in the United States that derivatives be subject to normal bankruptcy procedures."[8]

A staple of crime detective stories—and a feature of some real-life crimes as well—is the criminal who hides in plain sight. Rather than fleeing, the criminal stays near the crime scene, perhaps helping the detectives as they search for evidence and try to unravel the crime. If it works, no one suspects the criminal, because he seems to have nothing to hide. It doesn't occur to the investigators that their most energetic helper might be the same person they are looking for.

As the financial chaos of 2008 unfolded, ISDA's contributions sometimes reminded me of those detective stories. The inability to stop the derivatives and repo creditors of Bear Stearns, AIG, and Lehman from terminating their contracts if any of these companies filed for bankruptcy complicated their options when the financial crisis hit, diminishing the virtues of a bankruptcy resolution. Bankruptcy still would have been preferable to an ad hoc bailout, as we saw in Chapter 2. But the derivatives exemptions remove an important benefit.

The International Swaps and Derivatives Association—representing Goldman Sachs, JPMorgan Chase, Citigroup, and other major participants in the derivatives markets—had vigorously campaigned for precisely these exclusions. Yet ISDA proclaimed itself as the solution to, rather than the source of, the problem. After Lehman filed for bankruptcy, ISDA established a protocol for coordinating and reducing the claims from contracts terminated by Lehman's derivatives creditors, then applauded its efforts to help limit the fallout from Lehman's bankruptcy filing.

Although ISDA's hands were not altogether clean in the 2008 crisis, several concerns raised by it and other defenders of special treatment for derivatives do need to be taken seriously. Two in particular stand out—each highlighting the consequences of delay in a high-volatility market like derivatives. The first involves derivatives counterparties that have a large hedging transaction with the troubled bank. Suppose Energy Company has entered into a $100 million currency swap with Bank of the World, which Energy needs for protection against the possibility that changes in the exchange rate will affect the earnings of its foreign subsidiary. If BOW filed for bankruptcy and its swaps were subject to the normal bankruptcy rules, Energy might find itself dangerously in limbo. The automatic stay would prevent Energy from terminating the swap and entering into a new swap, to make sure that it remained protected. To be sure, Energy could go ahead and purchase the second swap, just to be safe. But if Energy does this, it will be stuck paying for two contracts, not just one, if BOW chooses to go through with the original contract. If the swaps are costly, buying the second swap may not be a realistic option.

The second concern is that the value of derivatives contracts is extremely volatile, and can change considerably over a short period of time. This, too, could make a derivatives buyer like Energy vulnerable. Suppose that BOW filed for bankruptcy at a time when BOW would owe $500,000 under their currency swap if the contract were closed out, because the foreign currency has declined in value; and BOW has posted securities worth $300,000 to secure any obligations. Two months later, however, the dollar has risen in value, so that Energy will now owe BOW money if the contract is terminated. Or BOW still owes Energy $500,000 but the value of the securities posted by

BOW has fallen to $100,000. Either way, the delay is costly to Energy, and the stay prevents Energy from doing anything about it.

Another version of this second argument, which is often put to me in conversation by Darrell Duffie, the leading derivatives economist (my reliance on his work will be evident from the citations in this book), focuses on repo transactions. Because repo transactions are extremely short-term—often lasting a single day—holding them up even temporarily could be devastating to the market.

The first thing to note is that many creditors could limit these risks simply by being careful with their contracting. (I ignore for the moment the beneficial effect the new clearinghouses may have; I'll consider them later.) If a derivatives user like Energy Company needs to take a huge hedging position, it should probably buy several smaller derivatives with different banks, rather than buying one huge position. With the second concern—volatile values—Energy can limit its exposure by requiring BOW to post adequate collateral. Moreover, bankruptcy itself addresses the danger that the value of Energy's collateral may fall during the case. Energy is guaranteed the full value that the collateral has as of the beginning of the case—here, $300,000—under a bankruptcy principle known as "adequate protection."[9]

Not only could creditors limit their exposure by being more careful about their derivatives contracting—encouraging them to do so is in fact a *benefit* of ending derivatives' special treatment—but the effect of ordinary bankruptcy treatment is not nearly so dramatic as many critics assume. I just mentioned one safeguard provided by the ordinary rules—protection of the value of a creditor's collateral as of the beginning of the case. The effect of ordinary treatment on repos also is much more limited than one might expect.

Under ordinary bankruptcy rules, a debtor like BOW is entitled to "assume" most ongoing contracts, as long as the debtor fixes any defaults and commits to satisfying all of its obligations for the remainder of the contract. But this power does not apply to loan transactions. Because repos are essentially loans to the debtor, BOW would not have the right to insist on continued performance. The contract would automatically be terminated. Thus, repo lenders would not need to worry about being trapped in a bankruptcy proceeding. If they were adequately collateralized, as they usually are, they would get what they were owed and could move on. (Thomas Jackson and I work through these and other examples in much more detail in a recent article, which may be of interest to those who wish to learn more about these and other bankruptcy nuances, such as the treatment of "netting" in bankruptcy.)[10]

Even careful contracting and existing bankruptcy protections do not make the concerns we have been discussing go away altogether. Derivatives creditors may still be exposed, even if they don't put all of their eggs in the same hedging baskets; and derivatives contracts are nothing if not volatile.

The most sensible response to these concerns is to limit the duration of the automatic stay so that a derivatives creditor like Energy Company is not in limbo for weeks or months. While there is no perfect duration, I would propose that the stay last for three business days. Three days—which is slightly longer than the one day provided in ordinary banking resolution and the one-plus day in a Dodd-Frank resolution—would give managers who have thought through their resolution strategy before filing for bankruptcy enough time to decide how to handle the company's derivatives and other assets, while limiting the exposure of its derivatives counterparties.

Even a very limited delay does have costs. In addition to the brief exposure a derivatives creditor like Energy Company would have after Bank of the World filed for bankruptcy, the *possibility* of a bankruptcy and a subsequent stay would increase the incentive for repo creditors and others to flee as Bank of the World declined into financial distress (another issue Duffie has identified). That is, removing the special treatment would affect the way creditors behaved before the bankruptcy filing. The prospect of even a tiny delay would increase, at least a little, the propensity for repos and derivatives creditors to initiate a run.

These costs are real. But the benefits of removing the special treatment are so great, particularly to the extent they enhance bankruptcy as an alternative to the new resolution framework, that they seem to me to far outweigh the costs of a limited stay and the application of other ordinary bankruptcy rules to these creditors.

I have deliberately postponed any discussion of the clearinghouses now required by Dodd-Frank to avoid putting too much weight on them in my analysis. It is too early to tell how large a percentage of the derivatives market will end up being cleared. If many derivatives like Energy Company's currency swap end up not getting cleared, nothing about the analysis thus far would change. But if the clearing requirement truly takes hold, as seems likely, it further strengthens the case for removing the special treatment of derivatives. If Energy's derivative is cleared, the clearinghouse will be responsible for backstopping BOW's performance. As a result, Energy would be fully protected, and the cost of either keeping the contract in place or replacing it would be borne by the clearinghouse.

The presence of the clearinghouse does raise another question, however. How should the clearinghouse be treated in bankruptcy? Should it be subject to the stay and the other ordinary bankruptcy rules, or should the clearinghouse be exempt? The Dodd-Frank resolution rules opt for exemption, explicitly excusing clearinghouses from any stay and instructing the FDIC to continue to honor margin and other requirements. While this approach may seem intuitively plausible, it would interfere with a financial institution's ability to arrange the most efficient resolution of its financial distress. Clearinghouses' demands for margin, or their termination of contracts, could disrupt resolution, just as similar demands by a counterparty would. If we want to make bankruptcy as effective as possible, we will need to apply the same three-day stay and the same ordinary bankruptcy rules to the clearinghouses as well as to derivatives creditors.

I have analyzed this very technical topic in extensive detail because so much is at stake. By restoring ordinary bankruptcy treatment for derivatives and other financial contracts, Congress could undo much of the damage of the Dodd-Frank resolution rules. The prospect of a stay, added to the other benefits of Chapter 11, would encourage the managers of troubled financial institutions to take matters into their own hands, preparing for financial distress and filing for bankruptcy long before lumbering regulators finally seize control under the Dodd-Frank resolution rules. It would not eliminate bailouts or resolution altogether, but it would make them less likely.

Among the many studies the Dodd–Frank Act has commissioned is a study on the efficacy of bankruptcy for resolving the financial distress of financial institutions. One can hope that proposing to reverse the special treatment of derivatives will be the principal recommendation the study makes.[11]

Other Bankruptcy Reforms for Financial Institutions

If Congress did nothing else, removing the special treatment for derivatives in bankruptcy would undo a considerable amount of the damage of the Dodd–Frank resolution rules. The prospect of a stay would give the managers of a troubled financial institution a reason to prepare for financial distress, rather than stalling in the hope of a bailout. It would increase the attractiveness of bankruptcy as an alternative to the ad hoc, unpredictable resolution rules.

If lawmakers wanted to further adapt bankruptcy to the distinctive qualities of financial institutions, several other reforms would also be in order. Two are of particular note.

The first would remove an anachronistic limitation on investment banks that file for bankruptcy. Under current law, the investment banking subsidiaries of an investment bank cannot file for Chapter 11, because the bankruptcy laws permit "brokerages" to file only under Chapter 7. If the investment banking subsidiary files for Chapter 7, its managers will be replaced by a trustee, who is required to liquidate its assets. (Under a parallel process, the liquidation also can be conducted by a regulator called the Securities Investor Protection Corporation.)[12]

The decision to exclude brokerages from Chapter 11 once made a certain amount of sense. The exclusion was based on a concern for the protection of customer accounts and a perception that the rules governing the accounts would make a Chapter 11 proceeding costly and complicated. Better, the reasoning went, to just shut everything down.

But the exclusion is based on a world that no longer exists—the investment banks of the past. In the 1960s, investment banks were set up as simple partnerships, and focused primarily on brokerage and advisory services. But investment banks now look radically different. After the wave of initial public offerings of the past several decades, they are now publicly held corporations that rely much more on proprietary trading for their profits and are part of a network of related corporations. There is no reason to allow the other entities to file for Chapter 11, but not the brokerage operations.

When Lehman Brothers filed for bankruptcy in 2008, it easily skirted the exclusion from Chapter 11, as Drexel Burnham Lambert had done nearly two decades earlier. Lehman's holding company and some of its subsidiaries filed for Chapter 11, but the principal brokerage subsidiary did not file for bankruptcy at all, at least initially. (As this statement suggests, a company can put some of its subsidiaries in bankruptcy but not others if it wishes.) In order to use the bankruptcy proceedings to sell its North American brokerage operations to Barclays, Lehman started a liquidation proceeding for them a few days later, at the same time as the sale.

As the Lehman sale suggests, the exclusion from Chapter 11 can be circumvented. But there are questions whether this can be squared with the current bankruptcy rules. The bankruptcy judge in Lehman made clear, for instance, that he approved the sale because of the extraordinary urgency of the case, and might not do the same thing in the future. "I know that I need to approve this transaction," Judge Peck said. "But I also know that this is so exceptional . . . that it could never be deemed a precedent for future cases unless someone could argue that there is a similar emergency. It's hard for me to imagine a similar emergency."[13]

Rather than forcing bankruptcy lawyers to devise clever strategies for circumventing a rule that no longer makes sense, and hoping that the bankruptcy judge will approve, lawmakers would do well to remove the exclusion from Chapter 11.

A second adjustment would create a pool of specially selected judges to handle financial institution bankruptcies. Under one version of this approach, the Chief Judge of the Supreme Court would designate a group of federal district court judges, and each bankruptcy case involving a financial institution would be randomly assigned to one of these judges. The goal would be to assure that financial institution bankruptcies are handled by judges who have particular knowledge of and expertise with financial institutions.

A group of scholars coordinated by the Hoover Institution is currently drafting a proposed set of provisions designed with financial institution bankruptcies in mind. The proposal, which recommends that a new Chapter 14 be added to the bankruptcy laws, addresses the issues I have just described and several others. The project is quite promising (full disclosure: I am one of the members).[14] But a single key reform would provide the most important benefits: reversing the special treatment of derivatives.

Plugging the Chrysler Hole in Bankruptcy

My final reform proposal harkens back to our discussion of the Chrysler and General Motors bankruptcies in Chapter 2. Its goal is to prevent a repeat, by the government or by other insiders, of the government's abuse of bankruptcy in the carmaker bailouts.

A government repeat isn't hard to imagine. Suppose a major supplier to the auto industry fell into financial distress, as Delphi did a few years ago, or perhaps even Ford, the one carmaker that wasn't bailed out this time around. After watching how the government handled Chrysler and General Motors, investors won't get anywhere near a major firm in an important industry that is in financial distress, for fear that they would face the same fate as the senior lenders of Chrysler. The inability of an important firm to raise funds under distress conditions will put even more pressure on the government to step in with funding. The earlier bailouts have thus made future bailouts more likely, and the government will be tempted to try the same strategy it used with Chrysler and GM, commandeering the process and combining economic objectives with political ones.

Even worse, this alien intervention could infect bankruptcies that do not involve the government. Neither bankruptcy judge said, as the bankruptcy judge in Lehman and the Supreme Court in *Bush v. Gore* did, that the ruling was limited to the extraordinary circumstances in which the decision was made. Insiders in other cases can therefore try the same trick. The managers of a troubled company can strike a deal in which a lender—say a hedge fund or an equity fund—arranges to finance the company's operations during bankruptcy and to purchase all of its assets at a bargain-basement price, while also agreeing to carry over a few favored creditors. If they are worried that competing bidders might emerge, they can simply ask the court to impose "qualified bid" requirements that make it impossible for anyone else to bid, like the ones used with Chrysler and GM.

I do not mean to suggest that companies should never be permitted to sell assets—even the entire company—in bankruptcy. Sales are often essential to preserving as much of the value of the company as possible. The problem comes when the sale is really a disguised way of reorganizing the company without giving creditors their voting rights and other procedural protections.

The one safeguard that can prevent this abuse of the bankruptcy process is bankruptcy judges themselves. The bankruptcy judge can refuse to let a company sell assets in bankruptcy without a full and fair auction, for instance. With Chrysler and GM, the judges could have insisted on a longer auction period, and could have refused to allow bidding restrictions that discouraged competing bidders from making alternative bids for part or all of the company. The bankruptcy laws give the bankruptcy judge almost complete discretion whether to allow a sale to go forward.

This complete discretion stands in sharp contrast to the bankruptcy judge's discretion in other contexts, which is nearly always constrained. When the company proposes a formal reorganization plan, the bankruptcy judge is given a total of 16 different requirements that the plan must satisfy before it can be approved. With a sale, by contrast, prior cases provide only the most general guidance and the bankruptcy statute itself has almost none.

The great irony—which bankruptcy judges often muse about at professional events—is that this unfettered discretion can become a straitjacket—no discretion at all—in practice. When companies are in financial distress, they usually are desperate for cash to fund their operations, and lenders are of course well aware of this. Lenders increasingly insist that the debtor obtain approval of the proposed loan as soon as the company files for bankruptcy. In ordinary cases, this can complicate life for the bankruptcy judge but it does not create serious harm. But a lender that also wants to buy the debtor's assets may insist that both the loan and the sale be approved on a very short time line. If they aren't, the lender says, it will pull the plug and withhold funding, and the company will collapse. The lender may use this strategy to try to acquire the company's assets on the cheap.

These cases put the bankruptcy judge in a very difficult position. The two parties standing before the judge—the managers and the lender—both say the transaction is the only way to preserve the value of the company's assets, and that there is no time to spare in deciding. If the judge insists on more time or major changes to the terms of the proposed sale, the lender may make good on its threat to cut off funding. Although the judge theoretically has complete discretion whether to approve the loan and proposed sale, in reality there is very little discretion if the threat is credible. When the government stepped in as the lender in the Chrysler and GM cases and made these same kinds of threats, it put the bankruptcy judges in an almost impossible position. Calling the bluff would have meant thumbing their noses at the U.S. government.

A simple reform would address the most egregious of these cases—cases like Chrysler in which the government used a sham sale to restructure the company—by putting constraints on the bankruptcy judge's discretion. Rather than having unlimited discretion whether to approve a sale, this proposal (developed in work with Harvard Law Professor Mark Roe) would forbid a company from using the bankruptcy sale provision to sell its assets if more than half of the stock or more than half of the debt of the buyer will be held by creditors or stockholders of the old company. (In Chrysler, more than 80 percent of the obligations were carried over and in GM the percentage was just as high.) These cases are really reorganizations and should be subject to the safeguards that Chapter 11 provides for a corporate reorganization.[15]

This rule would plug the hole in our bankruptcy laws that was created by the government's decision to commandeer bankruptcy for its Chrysler and GM bailouts. In cases that really are reorganizations, the parties would be steered away from the sale provision and back into the ordinary Chapter 11 process. Future Chryslers would be prevented, and the rule-of-law virtues of the bankruptcy process would come fully into play.

Bankruptcy to the Rescue

It is tempting to respond to the government-bank partnership and the reliance on ad hoc intervention by calling for repeal of the Dodd-Frank Act, as some have done. But this is a mistake, both because parts of the legislation are a genuine improvement and because even limited repeal is, as they say in Washington, a nonstarter.

A better response is to look for opportunities to bring market actors and rule-of-law principles back into the picture in an era that will be defined by government regulation. From this perspective, bankruptcy is an obvious hunting ground. It has all of the rule-of-law virtues that are subverted at key points in Dodd-Frank, particularly for systemically important financial institutions that are in financial distress. The simple changes that I have proposed would not require even one-hundredth of the pages filled by Dodd-Frank, yet they would take a big step toward a more balanced and effective regulatory framework.

Chapter 10

An International Solution?

I f Bank of the World (BOW)—our hypothetical bank with major
outposts in China and India, and perhaps links to Japan and Europe
as well—collapses and the Federal Deposit Insurance Corporation
(FDIC) is appointed as receiver under the Dodd-Frank Act, what happens to those offices around the world? Do they simply go on their own
merry way, more or less unaffected by the travails at BOW's New York
headquarters? Or do they become part of a single resolution proceeding
that spans the globe, with the FDIC overseeing its multiple parts?

The answer is neither. If you imagined that a separate foreign subsidiary might be immune to the collapse of its American headquarters,
at least if the subsidiary is itself healthy, just talk to anyone who worked at
Lehman's Asian subsidiaries, three of which shut down as a result of the
Lehman default. And if you imagined a smooth, worldwide insolvency

provision, a quick survey of any cross-border insolvency would quickly disabuse you of this notion (unless you're an insolvency scholar; the scholarly literature teems with elegant proposals for a harmonious worldwide procedure, as we will see). The cross-border cases to date— both financial institutions and cases involving other businesses—have been messy and often contentious, with a separate insolvency proceeding and separate set of insolvency rules for every country in which the debtor has assets.

The question of how to manage the failure of a worldwide company—especially but not only systemically important financial institutions—has bedeviled regulators and diplomats for as long as the world has been "flat." The Dodd-Frank Act doesn't even pretend to provide a comprehensive solution to these issues. Indeed, given the global reach of the crisis, it is remarkable how limited Dodd-Frank's contributions are in these areas.

In the drafters' defense, there won't ever be a truly worldwide solution to the distress of systemically important financial institutions. The best we can hope for is incomplete solutions and partial coordination. Dodd-Frank makes several minor contributions in this pragmatic spirit (as well as employing at least one strategy with a hint of xenophobia that could prove very counterproductive). In addition to pointing out some of the gaps, I will argue in this chapter that more can be done through simple strategies such as a limited treaty, as well as by addressing some of the problems with Dodd-Frank's domestic regulation that we have talked about throughout the book.

Basic Framework

Here, in summary form, are some of the key features we will be considering:

- FDIC coordination with foreign regulators.
- Ban on foreign traders or brokers from countries with inadequate regulation.
- "Living wills."

The Dodd–Frank Act's efforts to address the international dimensions of financial regulation are thin, to put it kindly. But the Act does deal with international concerns in three ways.

The legislation's first strategy is simply to encourage cooperation between U.S. regulators and their foreign counterparts. It authorizes the FDIC to enter into cooperation agreements with foreign regulators, and invites the Public Company Accounting Oversight Board to share confidential information obtained in its oversight of accounting firms. The Act's second strategy is a remarkable threat to ban brokers and derivatives traders from the U.S. markets if their country's regulation poses a threat to "the stability of the United States financial system." These provisions are apparently designed to punish countries that might lure derivatives trading away from the United States through the promise of less intrusive regulation, as the United Kingdom did in the 1990s and early 2000s. The final contribution is a new requirement that systemically important financial institutions prepare a "living will" outlining a plan "for rapid and orderly resolution in the event of material financial distress or failure." Although the living will requirement is not explicitly aimed at international concerns, forcing the largest financial institutions to explain their structure and their fire-escape plans could prove to be Dodd–Frank's most enduring contribution to international coordination.[1]

Before examining the new Dodd–Frank approach, its limitations, and related issues in more detail, this chapter first considers why the largest financial institutions have become so complex and difficult to manage, particularly when they fail.

Problems of Cross-Border Cases

In one sense, it's obvious why the financial distress of a systemically important institution like Bank of the World is so messy in its worldwide dimensions. The failure of an institution that is so complicated and far-flung will inevitably cause convulsions. Complexity is indeed one of the most vexing issues, but there are several very different difficulties as well. To develop even partial solutions to the problems of cross-border insolvencies, and to think about how best to regulate their cross-border dimensions while they are still healthy, we need to identify the root causes.

Start with the complexity and opacity of the largest financial institutions. One measure of just how complex they are is the number of separate entities they have. As of several years ago, Citigroup clocked in at 2,435 different legal entities (separate corporations, trusts, and partnerships), all in the same corporate family. Lehman had several thousand entities when it filed for bankruptcy in 2008. The other systemically important institutions are similarly complex.[2]

There is no single explanation why these financial behemoths can't seem to stop adding to their collections of separate businesses. The first of at least four sources of complexity, ironically enough, is that putting different businesses in different entities simplifies the bank's own internal risk management. If different pieces of the business are in separate boxes, the performance and problems of each are less likely to get blurred, which may make it easier for managers to monitor them. The customers of a financial institution may also prefer that certain businesses be kept separate. Even in countries that permit the same subsidiary to conduct both commercial and investment banking operations, banks often separate them (as is required in the United States) to reduce concerns about conflicts of interest in the responsibilities of the two parts of the business (as when the commercial bankers make loans to a business in the hope that the business will provide investment banking work for the investment bankers).[3]

Another source of complexity is mergers. In the article from which much of this discussion is drawn, Jacopo Carmassi and Richard Herring recount the growth of JPMorgan Chase through a vortex of merger activity. In 1991, Chemical Bank and Manufacturers Hanover merged, starting the corporate snowball rolling. Chemical Bank, which was nearly twice as large after the merger as before, merged with Chase Manhattan Bank in 1996. Four years later, this bank merged with J.P. Morgan & Company, ultimately forming JPMorgan Chase & Company. In 2004, JPMorgan Chase merged with Bank One (in the transaction that brought Jamie Dimon, the current CEO, into JPMorgan. In 2008, JPMorgan added two more banks to its collection,

Bear Stearns and Washington Mutual. With each acquisition came a slew of new entities.[4]

Two final reasons for complexity are taxes and maneuvering around other regulations. Both tax and regulatory factors may encourage a bank to set up special purpose vehicles for particular transactions, for instance. The special entity will stand on its own bottom, so to speak, both for tax purposes and in the event of financial distress of the parent corporation. Banks also have always used separate entities to take advantage of loopholes in existing regulations. In the past, for instance, they used separate entities to evade usury restrictions on their credit card business or geographical limitations on expansion.[5]

The sheer number of entities, and the diversity of reasons for their proliferation, makes sorting out a giant financial institution's activities daunting even under the best of circumstances. But the complexity is magnified by another factor: The largest financial institutions routinely conduct their business around the world in ways that ignore the legal structure of the institution.

Nowhere does this confusion between business and legal structure rear its head so often as in the distinction between branches and subsidiaries. Unlike a subsidiary, a branch is not a separate legal entity. If Bank of the World, the American parent company, starts a branch bank in California and another branch in Tokyo, these branches are each simply part of the parent corporation as a legal matter. Their assets are BOW assets, and their liabilities are part of the larger mass of BOW liabilities. If Bank of the World sets them up as subsidiaries, by contrast, the California and Tokyo offices are separate corporations. The assets and liabilities of each subsidiary are its own, distinct from those of each other and from Bank of the World. Despite the stark legal differences between branches and subsidiaries, large financial institutions often ignore the boundaries. They treat separate subsidiaries as if they are part of Bank of the World, or treat branches as if they were separate corporations. The disconnect between business and legal structures adds further complexity to institutions that already don't suffer from a lack of it.

In addition to complexity and opacity, the second way that the failure of a systemically important financial institution can wreak havoc is through disruption to clearing, settlement, and general cash flow services, both outside and within the troubled institution itself. The collapse of Bankhaus Herstatt in 1974, which is often mentioned as the first cross-border financial institution collapse of the current era, had an impact on clearing and settlement that was disproportionately disruptive given the relatively small size of the bank. "When the German supervisor found that it was insolvent," according to Richard Herring,

> it was closed at the end of the German business day, which was during the middle of the clearing and settlement process at the Clearing House Interbank Payments System in New York, where the dollar leg of most large-value foreign exchange transactions is settled. The consequence was that several institutions that had sold European and Asian currencies to Herstatt earlier in the clearing day, [with] the expectation of receiving dollars, found that they had unexpectedly become claimants in a German bankruptcy proceeding that extended for decades. [This] caused the largest foreign exchange market at the time (the dollar/Deutsche-mark market) to nearly collapse for several months.[6]

Lehman's bankruptcy caused similar convulsions within the Lehman network. Like many large firms, Lehman required that all of the cash of all of its entities be routed through a cash management system in New York. When Lehman was dumped into bankruptcy by the U.S. government, its foreign subsidiaries were cut off from their cash while Lehman and its lawyers scrambled to determine who was entitled to what. The delay was crippling for three Asian subsidiaries, which closed down and then were sold to Nomura Holdings during the period of uncertainty.[7]

The final set of problems comes from the cross-border component of cross-border insolvencies. If Bank of the World has offices in 10 different countries, it will be subject to 10 different insolvency frameworks. There is no worldwide insolvency framework, and even if there were we could be sure that many countries would refuse to follow it. When a large institution like Bank of the World fails, the first response of the regulators in most countries is to start a local proceeding and pull all the assets they can get their hands on into that proceeding. The existence of separate proceedings makes coherent resolution nearly impossible, particularly given the often dramatic differences among the jurisdictions' insolvency rules. Even two countries as similar as the United States and England may have sharply inconsistent approaches to a core insolvency question. In the United States, for instance, creditors can be forced to give back payments they received during the 90 days before bankruptcy. While England has its own claw-back provision, its scope is much more limited and often does not require creditors to cough up their payments. This distinction was one of the delicate issues that had to be resolved when the newspaper empire Maxwell Communication Corporation filed for bankruptcy in the 1990s.

Each of these problems is enough to keep regulators and diplomats awake at night. Put all the problems together and it sometimes seems remarkable that regulators and diplomats haven't simply thrown up their hands.

Scholarly Silver Bullets

The initial scholarly literature on cross-border insolvency focused primarily on nonfinancial corporations. Most scholars argued for some version of a *universalist* approach. Under universalism, the insolvency laws of one country would apply throughout the world, to all of the proceedings. In a *territorialist* system, by contrast, each country applies its own laws to any property located within that country.

My favorite universalist solution for cross-border insolvencies was proposed by my friend Robert Rasmussen, one of the top bankruptcy scholars of the past several decades. Under Rasmussen's proposal— which he called a "menu approach"—a corporation would be required to select the insolvency laws that would apply in the event of a subsequent insolvency, and to identify its choice in the company's founding documents. The company could choose the laws of any nation it wished, even if it did not have any operations in that country. (Thus, the "menu" includes the insolvency laws of every country in the world.) Rasmussen argued that the menu approach would remove the frictions that come from the effort to coordinate multiple sets of insolvency rules, and that companies would tend to choose the insolvency laws that were most sensible for that particular company. If they didn't, the reasoning went—if a company, say, chose insolvency rules that made it impossible to dislodge lousy managers—investors would punish the company by paying less for its stock or charging more for credit.[8]

Rasmussen's menu approach has its own particular strengths and weaknesses as compared to other universalist proposals—more strengths than weaknesses, which is why it's my favorite of the bunch—but it shares one crushing debility with the others. Countries care about their sovereignty. And because they care deeply about their sovereignty, it is inconceivable that most or all nations would agree to be bound by whatever set of laws a multinational organization selected. Few would dissent from the proposition that applying a single set of insolvency rules would be preferable to the current welter of often conflicting rules. It would radically simplify the chaos of having to coordinate among numerous conflicting rules and claims to priority. But any realistic strategy needs to provide a role for territorialism— for allowing a nation to apply its own laws to the property located in that nation.

In recent years, the European Union has made genuine progress by working within these parameters. When a company with a cross-border presence falls into financial distress, EU rules provide for a main proceeding in the country where the debtor is headquartered, as well as ancillary proceedings in other countries where it has assets or operations. But the system is still being worked out, and it applies only to the nations that have committed themselves to the EU political network. Needless to say, a great deal of work remains to be done.[9]

Dodd-Frank's Contribution to Cross-Border Issues

If nothing else, the Dodd-Frank Act adds many words to the problem of handling the cross-border dimensions of a large financial institution's failure. The many words do not add up to anything like a solution. Instead, they are further evidence of just how intractable the problem is.

If you ran a computer word search for the word *foreign* through the entire Dodd–Frank Act, you would find that it turns up dozens and dozens of times—so frequently, in fact, that you would probably soon give up counting, as I did when I tried the exercise. Setting aside the references that are incidental to our present concerns, two main themes emerge: a plea for American regulators and their foreign counterparts to coordinate and cooperate, and a threat to exclude foreign brokers and other institutions from U.S. financial markets if their home country does not appropriately regulate its own financial institutions. These two themes, together with a provision we saw briefly in Chapter 8—the requirement that systemically important institutions prepare a living will—are Dodd–Frank's contribution to the problems of cross-border insolvency.

The plea consists of a series of invitations and instructions for American regulators to cooperate with their foreign counterparts. The new legislation explicitly authorizes the principal accounting regulator—the Public Company Accounting Oversight Board—to share information with its counterparts in other countries. And the resolution rules are peppered with invitations for the FDIC to communicate with its foreign counterparts throughout the resolution process. The legislation invites the FDIC to request foreign assistance, for instance, and authorizes it to enter into coordination agreements with foreign governments. The Securities and Exchange Commission (SEC) and Commodity Futures Trading Commission (CFTC) also are told to consult with their foreign counterparts as they develop the new rules for regulating swaps.[10]

It is not clear whether this first set of provisions adds much more than a general "sense of the Congress" that cooperation is a very good thing in cross-border cases. Probably the most important of the provisions is the explicit authorization for the Public Company Accounting Oversight Board to share confidential information, since confidentiality obligations are sometimes a serious impediment to communication between regulators. Perhaps the FDIC's right to enter into coordination agreements will loosen, at least a little, whatever fetters might otherwise complicate its efforts to negotiate with the regulators handling foreign proceedings. But these provisions could hardly be described as a dynamic new strategy for dealing with cross-border insolvencies.

The second set of regulations—the threats—also seem to have coordination in mind, but the implicit objective is quite different and their implications will be more explosive once they come to light— perhaps about the time you read this chapter.

The first of these remarkable provisions, entitled "Access to United States Financial Markets by Foreign Institutions," invites the SEC to refuse to register a foreign broker if it "presents a risk to the stability of the United States financial system" and the broker's home country has not "adopted, or made demonstrable progress toward adopting, an appropriate system of financial regulation to mitigate such risk." According to another, even more stunning provision, the SEC or CFTC, after consultation with the Treasury, can ban an entity from participating in the U.S. swaps markets if it hails from a country whose regulation of swaps "undermines the stability of the United States financial system."[11]

What were the drafters of Dodd-Frank trying to do with these provisions? The principal purpose isn't so much to protect the United States against financial instability—although this no doubt is a secondary aspiration—as to try to do something about the risk that the costs of compliance with Dodd-Frank will drive derivatives operations into other countries. In a sense, these provisions are a back-handed strategy for achieving international harmonization. Harmonization has been one of the most prominent strategies for improving our handling of cross-border insolvency issues. Over the past 20 years, the United Nations (through its United Nations Commission on International Trade Law [UNCITRAL] Projects), the International Monetary Fund, and the World Bank have all sponsored initiatives to develop best practices for insolvency law, or core principles that every bankruptcy or insolvency law should have. The initiatives assume that once the core principles are identified, a country can improve its insolvency laws by better conforming them to the principles. They also assume—and this is where Dodd-Frank's threats come in—that if different countries' insolvency laws gradually converge, cross-border cases will be less messy in the future. (Full disclosure: I have had small roles in some of these initiatives, though I generally have been skeptical of their efficacy.)

The new threat provisions are, in a sense, saying that unless other countries put regulations similar to Dodd-Frank in place, the United States will retaliate against their big banks or derivatives participants that want to do business in the United States. The message is "harmonize or else." In the trade context, this kind of behavior would likely get the United States hauled before the World Trade Organization. There is also a whiff of desperation in the strategy. It is hard to imagine the SEC denying, say, Credit Suisse access to the U.S. derivatives markets because the Swiss bank is not subject to comparably strict regulatory restrictions in its home jurisdiction.

New Living Wills

Dodd-Frank's final contribution to the dilemma of cross-border financial regulation is the one genuine advance. As we saw in Chapter 8, the new legislation requires every systemically important institution to submit a plan "for rapid and orderly resolution in the event of material distress or failure"—otherwise known as a wind-down plan or living will. Like the pleas and threats, the living will requirement is a procedural response to the problems posed by systemically important institutions rather than a substantive regulation. In a sense, it is simply a disclosure obligation, although it goes beyond disclosure in requiring that the institution's directors and managers devise a plan for its resolution in the event of financial distress.

Much of the promise of the living will requirement lies in the changes it will spur by the companies that are required to prepare one. If Bank of the World is a muddled web of several thousand different entities, the obligation to outline the company's complete structure as part of its living will could prompt its managers and directors to decide that it's time to simplify the structure. Simplification might mean paring away unnecessary entities. It might also mean taking more care that BOW's legal structure matches its business structure.

If the living wills do cause the largest financial institutions to simplify their capital structures, a variety of favors will follow. As Richard Herring has pointed out in his writings on living wills, a simplified financial institution may be easier for regulators to oversee and easier for the company's own directors to monitor. As he puts it, the companies may "reduce their risk exposures because of greater awareness of the board, more thorough analysis by supervisors, and greater discipline by creditors and counterparties."[12]

We mustn't get too carried away in our enthusiasm for living wills. As long as there are good economic reasons to create a profusion of separate entities—and the existing tax and regulatory benefits are very good reasons—the largest financial institutions will remain extremely complex. While Bank of the World might slim down to 750 or 1,000 entities, it probably won't drop to 100.

Only if Congress were to remove some of the benefits that inspire the creation of new entities would the number truly decline. Let me go on record as strongly favoring any initiative along these lines. But I'm not holding my breath as I wait for this kind of reform, and wouldn't encourage you to hold your breath, either.

A Simple Treaty Might Do

Earlier in the chapter, I identified three principal concerns in cross-border cases—complexity, disruption to clearing services, and divergent insolvency regimes. As we have just seen, Dodd-Frank's living will requirement may help to reduce the largest firms' complexity somewhat. But it will do much less to address the other two concerns, particularly the wide divergences in insolvency regimes.

It would be unfair to expect Dodd-Frank or any other legislation to solve these problems in a comprehensive way. A truly comprehensive solution is impossible, given each country's sovereignty interest in control of the property located within its jurisdiction. As I have already suggested, I am also somewhat skeptical of harmonization as a strategy, although a gradual, partial convergence of regulation around the world is quite possible and might help.

But more limited reforms might address some of the concerns that are neglected by Dodd-Frank. Perhaps the most urgently needed is a treaty that would address some of the immediate and crippling, but avoidable, cross-border issues that arose when Lehman filed for bankruptcy. The treaty might make clear, for instance, that the cash that the subsidiaries of a systemically important financial institution forward to the company's cash management system, as under Lehman's arrangement, belong to the entities that forward it, not to the parent corporation. Even under existing U.S. bankruptcy law, it is clear that the parent corporation has no ownership interest in the cash and is required to return it. But an explicit treaty providing for immediate release of the cash to foreign subsidiaries would remove any confusion.[13]

To address the kinds of settlement problems that arose in the Bankhaus Herstatt case and cloud the waters today, the treaty might also let basic settlement and clearing operations go forward after a major institution has defaulted.

Those who have even a passing familiarity with efforts to line up support for international treaties may be skeptical of the prospects for dealing with these issues through a treaty. Negotiating a treaty can take years, and lining up a critical mass of support often drags on even longer. Trying to assemble worldwide support for a cross-border insolvency treaty would indeed be a hopeless quest. Because a high percentage of international finance is centered in a handful of countries, however, a more limited treaty could prove surprisingly effective.

A treaty that included just six countries—the United States, the United Kingdom, Germany, France, Switzerland, and Japan—would capture a large majority of the world's cross-border banking activity. And history suggests that even a treaty that included only the United States and United Kingdom would be a sufficient prod. This was essentially how Basel I, the first international accord on banking regulation, was put in place. After the initial Basel I discussions petered out, the United States and United Kingdom began work on an Anglo-American accord on banking regulation. The plans for the Anglo-American accord seem to have catalyzed the broader discussion, with the Basel I process proceeding quickly to an accord from that point on.[14]

Risk of a Clearinghouse Crisis

We have focused throughout this chapter on crises involving large banks and other financial institutions. But what about the vulnerability of the clearinghouses that are now a central feature of the new derivatives framework?

Clearinghouses should be more stable than the clearing and settlement systems that were jeopardized by the collapse of Bankhaus Herstatt in 1974, given that clearinghouses make daily margin calls. Margin, though, as a percentage of a counterparty's exposure, cannot perfectly shield a clearinghouse from extreme volatility. Even a 50 percent margin on hundreds of billions of dollars in losses across a market would leave hundreds of billions of dollars in exposure for the clearinghouse. Although that much volatility in a single day is a rare event, consider the so-called flash crash of May 6, 2010, when the Dow Jones Industrial Average fell 600 points in 30 minutes. Even after an equally quick recovery, the stock index posted a net loss of $200 billion in value for the day. The Dodd-Frank reforms will help regulators track and react to the derivatives market, but derivatives inherently rely on movements in other markets. Only a globally comprehensive, real-time, not-yet-invented information system could forestall a network of clearinghouses from reacting to volatility in a major asset market, and in an extreme case possibly even failing.

One partial response to these kinds of problems might be for clearinghouses to link together across borders through *multilateral netting* of transactions. Under multilateral netting, major swap dealers could offset all of their derivatives gains and losses for a given day not just among counterparties but also among clearinghouses. The major derivatives banks will surely push for this kind of coordination, since it would significantly reduce and simplify the collateral they are required to post. But this solution could pose its own dilemma in the event of a crisis. A default by a major swap dealer could create chaos among the clearinghouses as they tried to determine how to allocate net loss from the collapse. Absent some kind of framework for allocating the loss, the default could lead to a game of international hot potato played out in a high-speed electronic trading context.

Dodd-Frank doesn't delve into any of these issues that could arise from the international dimensions of the clearinghouses. They, too, should figure in any treaty process.

Reinvigorating the Rule of Law

In addition to pursuing a treaty, the biggest contribution the United States could make is simply to remove the impediments that discourage managers from adequately preparing for a potential disaster. The new Dodd-Frank living will requirement is a productive step, since it now requires that managers think about insolvency. Managers of the largest financial institutions can no longer dismiss insolvency preparation out of hand as Lehman's Richard Fuld and General Motors' Rick Wagoner both did.

But managers still have a strong incentive to plan for distress as little as they can, and to avoid insolvency proceedings at all costs thanks to the new Dodd-Frank resolution rules. This was the problem that occupied our attention in Chapter 9, and it is just as important for cross-border concerns. Absent adjustments, regulators will be the ones deciding when it is time for the company to enter resolution, and any managerial preparations will be partial at best. Managers are still better off lobbying for a bailout.

The simple bankruptcy reforms we considered in Chapter 9 would make bankruptcy an even more attractive alternative to Dodd-Frank resolution, and would diminish the likelihood of more ad hoc governmental interventions in the next crisis. If one of our goals is encouraging international cooperation, bankruptcy is also a more attractive model than an ad hoc resolution in which the FDIC has sweeping authority to do almost anything it wants.

Conclusion

E schewing the divide-and-conquer strategy of the New Deal, the Dodd-Frank Act has established a partnership between the government and the largest financial institutions. There are two possible forms the partnership may take absent further reform, both of them ominous.

The first possibility is that the government will pacify the giant financial institutions. Regulators may indeed slap the "more stringent" regulation the Dodd-Frank Act calls for on systemically important financial institutions, subjecting them to tough capital requirements and vigilantly enforcing the Volcker Rule. "Adopted with fear of instability in mind," Peter Wallison warns, "all of these new restrictions will make it difficult for competition and risk taking to break out among banks, [bank holding companies], and the large non-bank financial firms that will fall under the Fed's regulatory umbrella." He envisions that the banks will be protected from failure while being "willing—in fact, eager—to do what the government wants." This is the kind of pacification that Adolph Berle envisioned for the largest U.S. corporations during the New Deal.[1]

The alternative possibility is that the giant financial institutions will fend off the toughest of the restrictions, dissuading regulators from truly strict capital requirements and circumventing the Volcker Rule. They still will be subject to the political whims of the administration and bank regulators, since the Dodd-Frank Act provides so many mechanisms for channeling political objectives through the financial sector. But they will retain the capacity to take significant risks. The banks rather than the government will have the upper hand in the new partnership.

My own prediction is that the largest financial institutions will outmaneuver regulators, and thus that the second scenario is the more likely outcome. The giant banks will insist, quite plausibly, that finance will move overseas if the Volcker Rule is applied too restrictively. There is no guarantee that one or the other scenario will permanently prevail, however. Even if I am right that the largest financial institutions will fend off any serious regulatory interference, the balance may shift in future administrations.

The problem is that Dodd-Frank limits the possibilities to these two options, both of which are pernicious. Either way, political policy will be channeled through the financial sector, and economic considerations will be subject to displacement by political ones. Under either scenario, innovation will be stifled and the systemically important banks will be able to borrow more cheaply than their smaller, would-be competitors.

The government-bank partnership also makes irresistible the temptation to respond to a crisis with an ad hoc, regulator-dominated solution. If a systemically important institution falls into financial distress, regulators' first response will be to bail it out, either by putting pressure on other systemically important institutions—just as regulators did when Long-Term Capital Management nearly failed in 1998, or when Bank of America was forced to buy Merrill Lynch in 2008—or by maneuvering around the limitations on Fed intervention. If they do invoke the new resolution rules, the Federal Deposit Insurance Corporation (FDIC) will bail out the key creditors.

What is missing is any meaningful role for private parties and the rule of law. The managers of a troubled financial institution will plump for a bailout, just as they did throughout the Panic of 2008. Why wouldn't they? Some creditors may monitor, but the most sophisticated ones—the clearinghouses and derivatives counterparties—know they will be protected in the event of a collapse.

I have been critical of the Dodd–Frank Act throughout the book, and I will continue to criticize the partnership it has established between the government and the biggest banks, the invitation for ad hoc intervention, and its undermining of general rule-of-law principles. But it does have a few good features, such as the new framework for regulating derivatives and the Consumer Financial Protection Bureau. And I do think the simple reforms in the last two chapters could undo much of the damage. If private parties are given more scope and more encouragement to use their superior information, rather than relying on regulators alone, some of the Dodd–Frank Act's worst flaws could be quickly remedied. This would improve the efficacy of domestic financial regulation, and would bring important international benefits as well.

Notes

CHAPTER 1 Introduction

1. Cohan, 2009; Sorkin, 2009.
2. The *Rolling Stone* article, with its famous quote in the first line, is Taibbi, 2009.
3. The reference to 36 bank holding companies having $50 billion in assets is based on Davis Polk & Wardwell LLP, July 21, 2010, p. 5.
4. The proxy access provision is in Dodd-Frank, Section 971, and the vote on executive compensation is in Dodd-Frank, Section 951.
5. The provision requiring removal of references to rated securities is in Dodd-Frank, Section 939.
6. The hedge fund registration requirement is in Dodd-Frank, Section 403.
7. Johnson and Kwak, 2010. For a succinct summary of Stiglitz's case for breaking up the giant banks, see Stiglitz, June 12, 2009.
8. Wallison, June 18, 2009.
9. Posner and Vermuele, 2007. Levitin makes a somewhat similar argument about bailouts in Levitin, 2011.
10. Paulson's memoir is Paulson, 2010.
11. E-mail correspondence from Peter Wallison to David Skeel, August 23, 2010. Wallison also made this assessment around the same time in a commentary, Wallison, 2010.

CHAPTER 2 The Lehman Myth

1. Sorkin, July 13, 2010, p. B1.
2. The discussion in this section draws on Skeel, June 29, 2009, and Ayotte and Skeel, 2010.

3. Johnson and Kwak, 2010, p. 163; Wessel, 2009, p. 2.

4. Paulson, 2010, p. 209. The limitation on Federal Reserve funding is in Section 13(3) of the Federal Reserve Act.

5. The table is from Ayotte and Skeel, 2010, p. 490, and the discussion that follows draws on pp. 490–491.

6. John B. Taylor, Testimony to Subcommittee on Commercial and Administrative Law, Committee on Judiciary, U.S. House of Representatives 2, October 22, 2009.

7. Ibid. The testimony draws on a book that came out the same year: Taylor, 2009, pp. 26–27.

8. Sorkin, 2009, pp. 214–215.

9. The quote is from Onaran and Helyar, January 2009, pp. 50, 58.

10. *Bloomberg*, January 2009, p. 62.

11. Summe, 2009, p. 87.

12. McCarken, December 29, 2008.

13. Hallman, December 2008, p. 85.

14. The intervention is chronicled in detail in Cohan, 2009, pp. 54–115.

15. The concept of government by deal comes from Davidoff and Zaring, 2010. The discussion in the text draws on Skeel, June 29, 2009.

16. The Paulson quote is reported in Jones, November 18, 2008.

17. The Supreme Court vacated the decision of the initial appellate court, then dismissed the appeal to the Supreme Court. "In re Chrysler," *United States Law Week*, December 14, 2009, p. 3359.

18. Rattner first chronicled the events in the paragraph that follows in Rattner, 2009.

19. The transaction is described in more detail in Roe and Skeel, 2010, p. 727.

20. This requirement and the Chrysler sale agreement are discussed in Roe and Skeel, 2010, p. 752.

21. The arguments in this paragraph and the paragraphs that follow are developed in much more detail in Roe and Skeel, 2010.

22. The bidding restriction can be found in the court order establishing the rules for the auction. Order, Pursuant to Sections 105, 363, and 365 of the Bankruptcy Code and Bankruptcy Rules 2002, 6004, and 6006, 2009 WL 1360869, p. 20.

23. The bankruptcy decision approving the General Motors sale is *In re Gen. Motors Corp.*, 407 B.R. 463 (Bankr. S.D.N.Y. 2009).

24. The New Deal bankruptcy reforms, which brought an end to the original Wall Street bankruptcy practice, are described in Skeel, 2001, pp. 109–127.

CHAPTER 3 Geithner, Dodd, Frank, and the Legislative Grinder

1. Becker and Morgenson, April 27, 2009. *on Geithner*

2. Geithner's speech is Geithner, February 10, 2009; the reaction is described in Andrews and Labaton, February 11, 2009.

3. For a table setting forth the results of the stress tests, see www.nytimes.com/interactive/2009/05/07/business/0507-bank-stress-test.html. The *Saturday Night Live* skit is described in Johnson and Kwak, 2010, p. 171.

4. 11 U.S.C. Section 1322(b)(2) permits the modification of most mortgages and security interests, but excludes mortgages on a debtor's primary residence. If this exclusion were deleted, a debtor would be able to reduce the mortgage to the value of the property if it is underwater.

5. Davis Polk, whose involvement in the original proposal is discussed later, provided very helpful analyses of this and subsequent proposals and bills; Davis Polk & Wardwell LLP, "Treasury's Rules of the Road for Regulatory Reform," March 30, 2009. The resolution regime discussed in the next paragraph is analyzed in Davis Polk & Wardwell LLP, "Treasury's Proposed Resolution Authority for Systemically Significant Financial Companies," March 30, 2009.

6. Becker and Morgenson, April 27, 2009.

7. Warren, 2007, p. 8; Bar-Gill and Warren, 2008. The Fed's conflict of interest is discussed in Warren, 2007.

8. Paletta, July 22, 2010, pp. A1, A16.

9. Plunkett's vigil is described in Paletta, July 22, 2010.

10. Testimony of Harvey R. Miller, October 22, 2009.

11. A client memo written by the law firm Davis Polk seems to have played an important role in shaping the attempt to incorporate bankruptcy principles into the legislation. Davis Polk & Wardwell LLP, Nov. 12, 2009.

12. Testimony of Assistant Secretary Michael S. Barr, October 22, 2009.

13. E-mail to David Skeel and two others, February 2, 2010 (the e-mail says "Bankruptcy" rather than "Banking"; this is a typo).

14. The rise and fall and rise of Volcker is recounted in Cassidy, July 26, 2010.

CHAPTER 4 Derivatives Reform

1. The concerns about credit default swaps on Bear Stearns are described in Morgenson, March 23, 2008. The AIG collapse is recounted in detail in Sjostrom, 2009, p. 943.

2. The provision calling for a study of Fannie Mae and Freddie Mac is in Dodd-Frank, Section 1074.

3. The debates over the futures markets—the "devils in their gambling hells"—are colorfully described in Fabian, 1999.

4. The historical discussion in this and the next several paragraphs is drawn from Chahar et al., May 2010, which provides detailed citations to relevant authorities.

5. Joint Statement by Treasury Secretary Rubin, Federal Reserve Board Chairman Greenspan, and Securities and Exchange Commission Chairman Levitt, May 7, 1998.

6. The credit derivatives data can be found at Office of Comptroller of Currency, U.S. Department of the Treasury, *Quarterly Report on Bank Trading and Derivatives Activities Third Quarter 2009*, p. 2.

7. Stout, 1999, p. 701.

8. The definitions of *swap* and *security-based swap* can be found in Dodd–Frank, Section 721(a)(2).

9. The definitions of *swap dealer* and *major swap participant* are also in Dodd–Frank, Section 721(a)(2).

10. The clearinghouses do not remove the exposure of a counterparty like Goldman altogether. In addition to the possibility the clearinghouse itself could fail, the clearinghouse is the one who will determine the value of Goldman's position if Bank of America defaults. Goldman thus runs the risk that its position will be undervalued.

11. For a caution about trying to clear every credit default swap by one of the leading experts on clearinghouses, see Pirrong, 2008–2009, p. 44.

12. Duffie, Li, and Lubke, January 2010 (citing commitment by the 15 major dealer banks).

13. E-mail correspondence from Professor Darrell Duffie, Stanford University, to David Skeel, August 29, 2010.

14. The right of a clearinghouse to reject accommodation with another clearing-house is in Dodd–Frank, Section 725(h).

15. The emergency reserve requirement is in Dodd–Frank, Section 725(c).

16. The Federal Reserves authority to provide financial support to clearinghouses is in Dodd–Frank, Section 806.

17. Bolton et al., May 2010.

18. The requirement that clearinghouses set adequate margin requirements is in Dodd–Frank, Section 725. The instruction that regulators promulgate conflict of interest rules is in Dodd–Frank, Section 726.

19. The swap data repositories are in Dodd–Frank, Section 728.

CHAPTER 5   Banking Reform

1. The Council's objectives are set forth in Dodd–Frank, Section 111.

2. Dodd–Frank, Section 113.

3. Wallison, June 18, 2009.

4. Johnson and Kwak, 2010, p. 80 (cheaper borrowing costs).

5. Geithner, August 2, 2010.

6. The quoted language is from Dodd–Frank, Section 165.

7. French et al., 2010. The quote is at p.72 and the recommendations are at pp. 71–74.

8. The Collins amendment is described in more detail in Davis Polk & Wardwell LLP, July 21, 2010, pp. 47–52.

9. Elliott, 2009, for example, finds that increased capital requirements have only a small impact on bank lending.

10. Dodd–Frank, Sections 115 (study), 163 (use of contingent capital).

11. For an excellent analysis of the contingent capital concept, see Duffie, 2009. Mark Flannery has been a leading advocate of this approach. See, for example, Flannery, 2005. Scholars proposed somewhat analogous stock cancellation schemes as an alternative to ordinary corporate bankruptcy in the 1990s, such as Bradley and Rosenzweig, 1992, and Adler, 1993. But the proposals have not had traction in that context.

12. Johnson and Kwak, 2010, p. 180.

13. Ibid., pp. 214–215 (caps on size); p. 222 (comparison to Roosevelt).

14. Investment banks' increasing dependence on proprietary trading is recounted in Morrison and Wilhelm, 2007.

15. The Volcker Rule is in Dodd–Frank, Section 619.

16. Lucchetti and Strasburg, July 6, 2010; Schwartz and Dash, August 25, 2010.

17. Lucchetti, Rappaport, and Strasburg, August 5, 2010.

18. Dodd–Frank, Section 622 (adding a new Section 14 to the Bank Holding Company Act of 1956). The concentration limit is Section 622(b). The exception discussed in the next paragraph is Section 622(c), and the Council study in the paragraph that follows is Section 622(e).

19. Dodd–Frank, Sections 121, 163.

20. The compensation provision is Dodd–Frank, Section 956.

21. Geithner, August 2, 2010.

22. Gorton's analogy between the role of the repo markets in the recent crisis and nineteenth century bank runs is developed in Gorton, 2009. Gorton subsequently developed the article into a book.

23. The Fed's authority to limit short-term debt is in Dodd–Frank, Section 165(g).

CHAPTER 6 Unsafe at Any Rate

1. The proverb is quoted in Psalm 118:22.

2. The articles are Warren, 2007, and Bar-Gill and Warren, 2008.

3. Warren, 2007, and Bar-Gill and Warren, 2008.

4. Skeel, 2000, p. 1093.

5. Sullivan, Warren, and Westbrook, 1989, 2000.

6. Warren and Tyagi, 2003.

7. Sullivan, Warren, and Westbrook, 1983. The quote appears at p. 1145.

8. The article surveying law professors' media involvement is Jacoby, 2004.

9. Nader, 1965; Warren, 2007.

10. Warren, 2007, p. 8.

11. The first quote in this paragraph appears at ibid., p. 9, and the second at ibid., p. 17.

12. Bar-Gill and Warren, 2008.

13. The appointment of the director of the Bureau is in Dodd-Frank, Section 1011, and the director's inclusion on the Council is in Dodd-Frank, Section 111.

14. The general powers of the Bureau are in Dodd-Frank, Section 1021; the auto loan exclusion is in Dodd-Frank, Section 1029.

15. Authority is transferred to the Bureau from the Fed and other regulators under Dodd-Frank, Section 1061.

16. The Bureau's funding is provided for in Dodd-Frank, Section 1017.

17. The limitation on the Bureau's authority over small banks is in Dodd-Frank, Section 1026.

18. The provision governing the quashing of a Bureau regulation is in Dodd-Frank, Section 1023.

19. Dodd-Frank, Section 1022 (rule making), Section 1053 (hearings and adjudication), Section 1054 (litigation).

20. Dodd-Frank, Section 1032 (model form).

21. *Marquette Nat'l Bank of Minneapolis v. First of Omaha Service Corp.*, 439 U.S. 299, 318 (1978); Dodd-Frank, Section 1027(o) (usury limit).

22. The provisions described in this paragraph are in Dodd-Frank, Section 1403.

23. Keys, Mukherjee, Seru, and Vig, 2010.

24. Dodd-Frank, Section 941.

25. DeBedts, 1964, especially pp. 81–82.

26. Elizabeth Warren, Leo Gottlieb Professor of Law, Harvard Law School, Testimony before the House Financial Services Committee on "Regulatory

Restructuring: Enhancing Consumer Financial Products Regulation," Wednesday, June 24, 2009.

27. Warren and Tyagi, *The Two-Income Trap*, 2003. The first quote is at p. 147 and the second at p. 148.

28. The data on credit card receivables is available at Nilson Report, 2009; and a list of the largest bank holding companies can be found at National Information Center, www.ffiec.gov/nicpubweb/nicweb/Top50Form.aspx.

CHAPTER 7   Banking on the FDIC

1. Testimony of Professor David A. Moss, October 22, 2009.

2. Testimony of Assistant Secretary Michael S. Barr, October 22, 2009.

3. The events discussed in this paragraph and the next, as well as the details about banking and S&L regulation, are described in greater detail in Skeel, 1998, p. 723.

4. The FDIC is given the authority to close a bank unilaterally, after consultation with the primary regulator, in order to protect the deposit insurance fund in 12 U.S.C. section 1821(c)(10).

5. The triggering requirements for the resolution regime are in Dodd-Frank, Section 203(b).

6. Hynes and Walt, 2009 (citing the figures for FDIC-insured deposit transfers and purchase and assumptions).

7. Depositor preference was enacted as part of the Omnibus Budget Reconciliation Act of 1993. The deposit percentages are from Hynes and Walt, 2009, p. 28.

8. E-mail correspondence from William F. Kroener III to Thomas Jackson (Jan. 8, 2010).

9. The closure data can be found in Hynes and Walt, pp. 28–29.

10. Banking expert Bert Ely has compiled a list of FDIC bank closings since 2007. He estimates the total losses at $73.4 billion. E-mail from Bert Ely to David Skeel, August 24, 2010 (with spreadsheet).

11. Hynes and Walt also discuss the plight of WaMu's subordinated bondholders; Hynes and Walt, 2009, pp. 41–43.

CHAPTER 8   Bailouts, Bankruptcy, or Better

1. I should note here that some scholars—most notably, New York University law professor Barry Adler—have argued that an insolvency regime that shuts down insolvent companies and sells them as scrap may sometimes be optimal, due to the incentives it creates prior to insolvency.

2. For a discussion of information contagion and counterparty contagion that draws conclusions similar to the arguments in this paragraph and the next, see Helwege, Summer 2009, p. 24; Helwege, April 2009.

3. The Treasury White Paper is U.S. Department of the Treasury, 2009. The proposal that Federal Reserve emergency lending require Treasury approval is at p. 79.

4. The revisions to the Federal Reserve's 13(3) powers are in Dodd-Frank, Section 1101.

5. The "arbitrary and capricious" standard of review is in Dodd-Frank, Section 202.

6. The triggering provision is in Dodd-Frank, Section 203(b). The definition of *financial company* comes in Dodd-Frank, Section 201(a)(11)(iii).

7. Dodd-Frank, Section 214.

8. The company's very limited bases for challenging a petition are set forth in Dodd-Frank, Section 202(a)(1)(A).

9. The 24-hour review is in Dodd-Frank, Section 202(a)(1)(A)(v).

10. The classic case construing the due process clause as requiring notice and an opportunity to be heard is *Mullane v. Central Hanover Bank & Trust Co.*, 339 U.S. 306 (1950).

11. The provision giving the debtor's managers the exclusive right to propose a reorganization plan, known as the exclusivity rule, is 11 U.S.C. Section 1121.

12. Dodd-Frank, Section 167(d) (windup plans).

13. The temporary invalidation of ipso facto clauses is in Dodd-Frank, Section 210(c)(8)(F).

14. The "all or nothing" requirement is in Dodd-Frank, Section 210(c)(11).

15. Dodd-Frank, Section 204(d) (authority to guarantee debts); Section 210(n) (10 percent funding).

16. Paulson's insistence on driving down the price of the Bear Stearns sale was first reported by Kate Kelly in the *Wall Street Journal*: Kelly, May 29, 2008, p. A1.

17. Dodd-Frank, Section 206.

18. Dodd-Frank's preference and fraudulent conveyance rules are in Dodd-Frank, Section 210(a)(11).

19. Dodd-Frank, Section 214.

20. The bridge bank provisions are in Dodd-Frank, Section 210(h). The potential use of bridge banks as a de facto reorganization is discussed in Baird and Morrison, 2010, pp. 13–14.

21. The quote is from Greene, 2010.

22. Skeel, 2001. The birth of corporate reorganization is recounted at pp. 48–70.

CHAPTER 9   Essential Fixes and the New Financial Order

1. I talk about Kennedy, Douglas, and Frank in much more detail elsewhere, as in Skeel, 2001 and Skeel, 2005.

2. I have been arguing for reform in a number of scholarly articles, starting with Partnoy and Skeel, 2007, pp. 1019, 1048–1050. Other scholars who have taken a similar position include Stephen Lubben and, more recently, Mark Roe. See, for example, Lubben, 2009, Lubben, 2010, and Roe, 2010.

3. The provisions discussed in this paragraph can be found in 11 U.S.C. Section 362 (automatic stay); Section 541(c) (invalidation of ipso facto clauses); Section 547 (preferences); Section 548 (fraudulent conveyances).

4. The special derivatives protections discussed in this paragraph can be found in 11 U.S.C. Section 362(b)(17) (exception from automatic stay); Section 560 (ipso facto clauses honored); Section 546(g) (protecting from preference or fraudulent conveyance attack).

5. Statement by Federal Reserve Board Associate General Counsel Oliver Ireland, 1999.

6. The point that the special treatment of derivatives will make them more attractive than traditional financing was first made in Edwards and Morrison, 2005, p. 90, but Edwards and Morrison concluded that it would not be problematic. I am less sanguine about the substitution than are Edwards and Morrison, as the text makes clear. But it is important not to overstate the extent to which bankruptcy's special treatment drove the increased use of repo-based financing. Because investment banks sought to increase their leverage in the 1990s and 2000s, debt financing was already more attractive than issuing equity. And repo financing is much simpler than a traditional secured loan, the most comparable debt alternative.

7. Roe, 2011, p. 7.

8. Mengle, 2010, p. 1ff. The quote is at p. 2.

9. A creditor's collateral is entitled to protection in bankruptcy under 11 U.S.C. Section 362(d)(1).

10. Jackson and Skeel, June 24, 2010. The bankruptcy rule authorizing a debtor to assume a contract is in 11 U.S.C. Section 365(a) and the prohibition on assuming loan contracts is in 11 U.S.C. Section 365(c)(2).

11. The legislation provides for studies of bankruptcy as a mechanism for handling financial institution distress in two different places: Dodd-Frank, Sections 202(e) and 216.

12. The brokerage exclusion is in 11 U.S.C. Section 109(d). The analysis of the exclusion in this paragraph and the next several paragraphs draws on a more detailed treatment in Skeel, 2009, pp. 3–6.

13. *In the matter of LBH Inc. et al.*, U.S. Bankruptcy Court for the Southern District of New York, Case No. 08-13555 (September 19, 2008). The quote comes from pp. 251–252. In describing the sale as "exceptional," Judge Peck is speaking of the short time frame and other extraordinary factors, as well as the simultaneous liquidation and sale of the brokerage.

14. Kenneth Scott is the head of the Chapter 14 group, and Thomas Jackson has been the principal drafter. Other participants include Darrell Duffie, Richard Herring, William Kroener, me, Kimberly Summe, and John Taylor.

15. Roe and Skeel, 2010, p. 727.

CHAPTER 10   An International Solution

1. Among the key cooperation provisions are Dodd Frank, Sections 752 and 981; the threatened bans are in Dodd-Frank, Sections 173 and 715; and the living will is in Dodd-Frank, Section 165(d).

2. The determination that Citigroup had 2,435 subsidiaries is from Herring and Carmassi, 2010.

3. These factors are discussed in ibid. at pp. 202–205.

4. Ibid., p. 211.

5. Ibid., pp. 212–216.

6. The quote about Herstatt comes from Herring, 2009, p. 143.

7. The effect of Lehman's collapse on its Asian subsidiaries is briefly discussed in Press Trust of India, Sept. 17, 2008.

8. Rasmussen, 2000, p. 2252.

9. The EU treatment of cross-border insolvency is discussed in more detail in Skeel, 2006, pp. 439, 451–461.

10. Dodd-Frank, Section 981 (PCAOB cooperation with foreign authorities); Section 210(a)(1)(N) (FDIC coordination with foreign authorities); Section 752 (SEC and CFTC coordination on swaps).

11. Dodd-Frank, Section 173 (access to U.S. financial markets); Section 715 (prohibition on swaps trader's entry).

12. Herring, 2009, p. 141.

13. The bankruptcy provision that would ensure return of a subsidiary's cash is 11 U.S.C. Section 541(a), which includes only property in which the debtor (here, the parent corporation) has an ownership interest in the debtor's estate.

14. The analysis of this paragraph and my account of Basel I are based on conversations with Richard Herring.

Conclusion

1. Wallison, 2010. The first quote is at p. 6 and the second at p. 2.

Bibliography

Adler, Barry E. "Financial and Political Theories of American Corporate Bankruptcy." *Stanford Law Review* 45 (1993): 311–346.

Andrews, Edmund L., and Stephen Labaton. "Geithner Details New Bank Rescue Plan." *New York Times*, February 11, 2009.

Ayotte, Kenneth, and David A. Skeel Jr. "Bankruptcy or Bailouts?" *Journal of Corporation Law* 35 (2010): 469–498.

Baird, Douglas G., and Edward R. Morrison. "Dodd-Frank for Bankruptcy Lawyers." Unpublished manuscript, 2010.

Bar-Gill, Oren, and Elizabeth Warren. "Making Credit Safer." *University of Pennsylvania Law Review* 157 (2008): 1–101.

Bebchuk, Lucian A. "A New Approach to Corporate Reorganization." *Harvard Law Review* 101 (1988): 775–804.

Becker, Joe, and Gretchen Morgenson. "Geithner, as Member and Overseer, Forged Ties to Finance Club." *New York Times*, April 27, 2009.

Bolton, Patrick, Xavier Freixas, and Joel Shapiro. "The Credit Ratings Game." Unpublished manuscript, May 2010.

Bradley, Michael, and Michael Rosenzweig. "The Untenable Case for Chapter 11." *Yale Law Review* 101 (1992): 1043–1095.

Chahar, Vijit, et al. "Retooling Corporate Governance for the Twenty-First Century." Unpublished manuscript, May 2010.

Cohan, William D. *House of Cards: A Tale of Hubris and Wretched Excess on Wall Street*. New York: Doubleday, 2009.

Davidoff, Steven M., and David Zaring. "Regulation by Deal: The Government's Response to the Financial Crisis." *Administrative Law Review* 61 (2009): 463–541.

Davis Polk & Wardwell LLP. "Summary of the Dodd-Frank Wall Reform and Consumer Protection Act, Enacted into Law on July 21." July 21, 2010, www.davispolk.com/files/Publication/7084f9fe-6580-413b-b870-b7 c025ed2ecf/Presentation/PublicationAttachment/1d4495c7-0be0-4e9a-ba77-f786fb90464a/070910_Financial_Reform_Summary.pdf.

Davis Polk & Wardwell LLP. "The House and Senate Debate Resolution Authority." Nov. 12, 2009.

Davis Polk & Wardwell LLP. "Treasury's Proposed Resolution Authority for Systemically Significant Financial Companies." March 30, 2009, www.davis polk.com/1485409/clientmemos/2009/03.30.09.resolution.authority.pdf.

Davis Polk & Wardwell LLP. "Treasury's Rules of the Road for Regulatory Reform." March 30, 2009, www.davispolk.com/1485409/clientmemos/2009/ 03.30.09.regulatory.reform.pdf.

DeBedts, Ralph. *The New Deal's SEC: The Formative Years*. New York: Columbia University Press, 1964.

Duffie, Darrell. "Contractual Methods for Out-of-Court Restructuring." In *Ending Bailouts as We Know Them*, edited by Kenneth E. Scott, George P. Shultz, and John B. Taylor. Stanford, CA: Hoover Institution Press, 2009.

Duffie, Darrell, Ada Li, and Theo Lubke. "Policy Perspectives on OTC Derivatives Market Infrastructure." *Federal Reserve Bank of New York Staff Reports*, January 2010.

Edwards, Franklin R., and Edward R. Morrison. "Derivatives and the Bankruptcy Code: Why the Special Treatment?" *Yale Journal on Regulation* 22 (2005): 91–122.

Elliott, Douglas J. "Quantifying the Effects on Lending of Increased Capital Requirements." Working paper prepared for the Brookings Institution, September 21, 2009.

Fabian, Ann. *Card Sharps and Bucket Shops: Gambling in Nineteenth Century America*. New York: Routledge, 1999.

Flannery, Mark J. "No Pain, No Gain? Effecting Market Discipline via 'Reverse Convertible Debentures.'" In *Capital Adequacy Beyond Basel: Banking, Securities, and Insurance*, edited by Hal S. Scott. Oxford: Oxford University Press, 2005.

French, Kenneth R., et al. *The Squam Lake Report: Fixing the Financial System*. Princeton, NJ: Princeton University Press, 2010.

Geithner, Timothy F. "Rebuilding the American Financial System." Speech presented at New York University Stern School of Business, August 2, 2010.

Gorton, Gary. 2009. "Slapped in the Face by the Invisible Hand." Prepared for the Federal Research Bank of Atlanta's 2009 Financial Markets Conference: Financial Innovation and Crisis, May 11–13, 2009.

Greene, Jenna. "FDIC's New Power to Dissolve Companies Raises Concerns." Law.com, September 7, 2010.

Hallman, Ben. "A Moment's Notice." American Lawyer, December 2008, 85.

Harper, Christine, et al. "Wall Street Stealth Lobby Defends $35 Billion Derivatives Haul." Bloomberg, August 31, 2009. www.bloomberg.com/apps/news?pid=newsarchive&sid=agFM_w6e2i00.

Helwege, Jean. "Financial Firm Bankruptcy and Systemic Risk." Regulation, Summer 2009, 24–29.

Helwege, Jean. "Financial Firm Bankruptcy and Systemic Risk." Unpublished manuscript, April 2009.

Herring, Richard J. "Wind-Down Plans as an Alternative to Bailouts: The Cross-Border Challenges." In Ending Bailouts as We Know Them, edited by Kenneth E. Scott, George P. Shultz, and John B. Taylor. Stanford, CA: Hoover Institution Press, 2009.

Herring, Richard, and Jacopo Carmassi. "The Corporate Structure of International Financial Conglomerates: Complexity and Its Implications for Safety and Soundness." In The Oxford Handbook of Banking. Oxford: Oxford University Press, 2010.

Hynes, Richard M., and Steven D. Walt. "Why Banks Are Not Allowed in Bankruptcy." Unpublished manuscript, 2009.

Jackson, Thomas, and David A. Skeel Jr. "Transaction Consistency and the New Finance in Bankruptcy." Unpublished manuscript, June 24, 2010.

Jacoby, Melissa B. "Negotiating Bankruptcy Legislation Through the News Media." Houston Law Review 41 (2004): 1091–1144.

Johnson, Simon, and James Kwak. 13 Bankers: The Wall Street Takeover and the Next Financial Meltdown. New York: Pantheon, 2010.

Jones, Wendy. "Paulson, Bernanke Testify, Get Grilled." First Read (NBC), Nov. 18, 2008. Available at http://firstread.msnbc.msn.com/_news/2008/11/18/4425489-paulson-bernanke-testify-get-grilled.

Kelly, Kate. "Bear Stearns Neared Collapse Twice in Frenzied Final Week." Wall Street Journal, May 29, 2008, A1.

Keys, Benjamin J., Tanmoy Mukherjee, Amit Seru, and Vikrant Vig. "Did Securitization Lead to Lax Screening? Evidence from Subprime Loans." Quarterly Journal of Economics, 2010, 307.

Lattman, Peter. "Judge Orders Auction in a Rebuke to Delphi Plan." *Wall Street Journal*, June 11, 2009, B1.

Levitin, Adam J., "In Defense of Bailouts." *Georgetown Law Journal* (forthcoming 2011).

Lubben, Stephen J. "The Bankruptcy Code without Safe Harbors." *American Bankruptcy Law Journal* 84 (2010): 123–142.

Lubben, Stephen J. "Derivatives and Bankruptcy: The Flawed Case for Special Treatment." *University of Pennsylvania Journal of Business Law* 12 (2009): 61–78.

Lucchetti, Aaron, Liz Rappaport, and Jenny Strasburg. "Gorman Hedges a Bet at Morgan." *Wall Street Journal*, August 5, 2010.

Lucchetti, Aaron, and Jenny Strasburg. "Banks Redefine Jobs of 'Prop' Traders." *Wall Street Journal*, July 6, 2010.

McCarken, Jeffrey. "Lehman's Chaotic Bankruptcy Filing Destroyed Billions in Value." *Wall Street Journal*, December 29, 2008.

Mengle, David. "The Importance of Close-Out Netting." *ISDA Research Notes*, 2010, 1.

Morgenson, Gretchen. "In the Fed's Crosshairs: Exotic Game." *New York Times*, March 23, 2008.

Morrison, Alan D., and William J. Wilhelm Jr. *Investment Banking: Institutions, Politics, and Law*. Cambridge: Cambridge University Press, 2007.

Nader, Ralph. *Unsafe at Any Speed: The Designed-In Dangers of the American Automobile*. New York: Grossman Publishers, 1965.

Nilson Report, August 2009. Available at www.creditcards.com/credit-card-News/credit-card-industry-facts-personal-debt-statistics-1276.php.

Onaran, Yalman, and John Helyar. "Lehman's Last Days." *Bloomberg Markets*, January 2009, 50, 58.

Paletta, Damian. "Fight over Consumer Agency Looms as Overhaul Is Signed." *Wall Street Journal*, July 22, 2010, A1, A16.

Partnoy, Frank, and David A. Skeel Jr. "The Promise and Perils of Credit Derivatives." *University of Cincinnati Law Review* 75 (2007): 1019–1051.

Paulson, Henry M., Jr. *On the Brink: Inside the Race to Stop the Collapse of the Global Financial System*. New York: Business Plus, 2010.

Pirrong, Craig. "The Clearinghouse Cure." *Regulation*, Winter 2008–2009, 44.

Posner, Eric, and Adrian Vermuele. *Terror in the Balance: Security, Liberty, and the Courts*. New York: Oxford University Press, 2007.

Press Trust of India, "3 Asian Subsidiaries of Lehman Brothers Suspend Operations." indianexpress.com, Sept. 17, 2008. Available at www.indianexpress.com/story-print/362386/.

Rasmussen, Robert K. "Resolving Transnational Insolvencies through Private Ordering." *Michigan Law Review* 98 (2000): 2252–2275.

Rattner, Steve. "The Auto Bailout: How We Did It." *Fortune*, October 21, 2009.

Roe, Mark J. "Bankruptcy's Financial Crisis Accelerator." *Stanford Law Review*, (forthcoming 2011).

Roe, Mark J., and David A. Skeel, Jr. "Assessing the Chrysler Bankruptcy." *Michigan Law Review* 108 (2010): 727–771.

Schwartz, Nelson D., and Eric Dash. "Despite Reform, Banks Have Room for Risky Deals." *New York Times*, August 25, 2010.

Sjostrom, William K., Jr. "The AIG Bailout." *Washington and Lee Law Review* 66 (2009): 943–991.

Skeel, David A., Jr. "Bankruptcy Boundary Games." *Brooklyn Journal of Corporate, Financial and Commercial Law* 4 (2009): 1–21.

Skeel, David A., Jr. "Creditors' Ball: The 'New' New Corporate Governance in Chapter 11." *University of Pennsylvania Law Review* 152 (2003): 917–949.

Skeel, David A., Jr. *Debt's Dominion: A History of Bankruptcy Law in America.* Princeton, NJ: Princeton University Press, 2001.

Skeel, David A., Jr. "European Implications of Bankruptcy Venue Shopping in the U.S." *University of Buffalo Law School* 54 (2006): 439–466.

Skeel, David. "Give Bankruptcy a Chance." *Weekly Standard*, June 29, 2009.

Skeel, David A., Jr. *Icarus in the Boardroom: The Fundamental Flaws in Corporate America and Where They Came From.* New York: Oxford University Press, 2005.

Skeel, David A., Jr. "The Law and Finance of Bank and Insurance Insolvency Regulation." *Texas Law Review* 76 (1998): 723–780.

Skeel, David Arthur, Jr. "Vern Countryman and the Paths of Progressive (and Populist) Legal Scholarship." *Harvard Law Review* 113 (2000): 1075–1129.

Sorkin, Andrew Ross. "Paulson Likes What He Sees in Overhaul." *New York Times*, July 13, 2010, B1.

Sorkin, Andrew Ross. *Too Big to Fail: The Inside Story of How Wall Street and Washington Fought to Save the Financial System—and Themselves.* New York: Viking, 2009.

Stiglitz, Joseph. "America's Socialism for the Rich." *Guardian*, June 12, 2009.

Stout, Lynn. "Why the Law Hates Speculators: Regulation and Private Ordering in the Market for OTC Derivatives." *Duke Law Journal* 48 (1999): 701–786.

Sullivan, Teresa A., Elizabeth Warren, and Jay Lawrence Westbrook. *As We Forgive Our Debtors: Bankruptcy and Consumer Credit in America.* Cambridge, MA: Harvard University Press, 1989.

Sullivan, Teresa A., Elizabeth Warren, and Jay Lawrence Westbrook. "Limiting Access to Bankruptcy Discharge: An Analysis of the Creditors' Data." *Wisconsin Law Review* (1983): 1091–1146.

Sullivan, Teresa A., Elizabeth Warren, and Jay Lawrence Westbrook. *The Fragile Middle Class: Americans in Debt.* New Haven, CT: Yale University Press, 2000.

Summe, Kimberly Anne. "Lessons Learned from the Lehman Bankruptcy." In *Ending Bailouts as We Know Them,* edited by Kenneth E. Scott, George P. Shultz, and John B. Taylor. Stanford, CA: Hoover Institution Press, 2009.

Taibbi, Matt. "The Great American Bubble Machine." *Rolling Stone,* July 9–23, 2009.

Taylor, John B. *Getting Off Track: How Government Actions and Interventions Caused, Prolonged, and Worsened the Financial Crisis.* Stanford, CA: Hoover Institution Press, 2009.

U.S. Department of the Treasury. *Financial Regulatory Reform: A New Foundation,* June 17, 2009, www.financialstability.gov/docs/regs/FinalReport_web.pdf.

U.S. Department of the Treasury. *Quarterly Report on Bank Trading and Derivatives Activities, Third Quarter 2009.* 2010, 2, www.occ.treas.gov/ftp/release/2009-161a.pdf.

Wallison, Peter J. "The Dodd-Frank Act: Creative Destruction, Destroy," *American Enterprise Institute Outlook,* August 31, 2010.

Wallison, Peter J. "Too Big to Fail, or Succeed." *Wall Street Journal,* June 18, 2009.

Warren, Elizabeth. "Unsafe at Any Rate." *Democracy,* Summer 2007, 8–19.

Warren, Elizabeth, and Amelia Warren Tyagi. *The Two-Income Trap.* New York: Basic Books, 2003.

Wessel, David. *In Fed We Trust: Ben Bernanke's War on the Great Panic.* New York: Crown Business, 2009.

Acknowledgments

A lthough long in gestation, this book was written quickly due to the press of events. Despite this, or perhaps because of it, I ran up major debts in a very short period of time. My research team—Albert Lichy, Spencer Pepper, and Paul Vogelman—read multiple drafts of the manuscript and provided assistance and insights of all kinds. I received detailed comments and suggestions from Colleen Baker, Peter Conti-Brown, Steven Davidoff, Dan Geldon, Randy Guynn, Marc Hecht, Adam Levitin, Nelson McKinley, Ken Scott, David Skeel Sr., Kimberly Summe, and Bob Thompson. Douglas Baird, Magda Bianco, Martin Bienenstock, Patrick Bolton, Silvana Burgese, Eric Dillalogue, John Douglas, Bill Draper, Darrell Duffie, Bert Ely, Mike Fitts, Courtney Geduldig, Harvey Miller, Frank Partnoy, David Payne, Merle Slyhoff, Elizabeth Warren, and Gary Witt contributed crucial help of various kinds; and the University of Pennsylvania Law School was generous with research support. I am grateful to all of you.

This book might never have been written if I hadn't gotten an e-mail from my editor, Laura Walsh, a few weeks before the Dodd-Frank Act was enacted. My thanks to Laura, Mary Daniello, Judy Howarth, Adrianna Johnson, and everyone at John Wiley & Sons.

For my wife Sharon and sons Carter and Stephen, who endured the lost spring and summer of 2010, I hope to thank you in other ways.

About the Author

David Skeel is the S. Samuel Arsht Professor of Corporate Law at the University of Pennsylvania. The author of *Icarus in the Boardroom: The Fundamental Flaws in Corporate America and Where They Came From* and *Debt's Dominion: A History of Bankruptcy Law in America*, he is a frequent speaker and commentator on corporate and financial issues. His commentary has appeared in the *New York Times, Wall Street Journal, Weekly Standard, Books & Culture,* and elsewhere.

Index